The
HEALTHY
HOUSEPLANTS
HANDBOOK

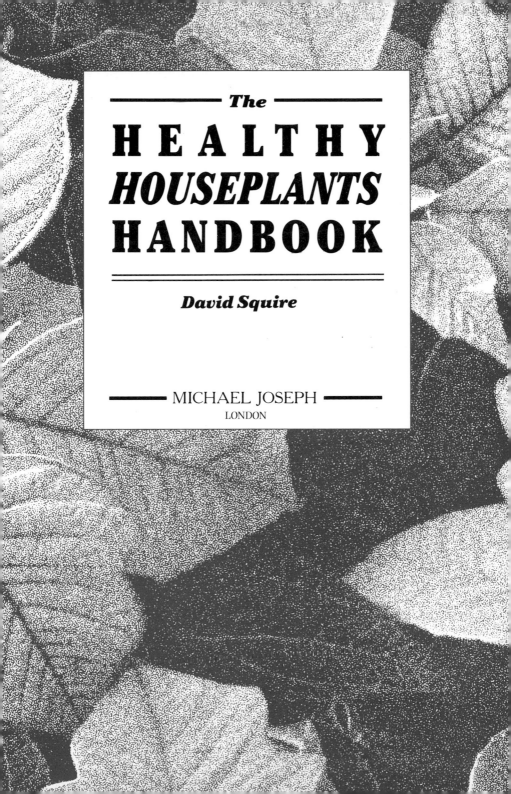

The
HEALTHY
HOUSEPLANTS
HANDBOOK

David Squire

MICHAEL JOSEPH
LONDON

MICHAEL JOSEPH
Published by the Penguin Group
27 Wrights Lane, London W8 5TZ, England
Viking Penguin Inc., 40 West 23rd Street,
New York, New York 10010, USA
Penguin Books Australia Ltd, Ringwood,
Victoria, Australia
Penguin Books Canada Ltd, 2801 John Street,
Markham, Ontario, Canada L3R 1B4
Penguin Books (NZ) Ltd, 182–190 Wairau Road,
Auckland 10, New Zealand

Penguin Books Ltd. Registered Offices:
Harmondsworth, Middlesex, England

First published 1988
Copyright © Marshall Editions Ltd 1988

British Library Cataloguing in Publication Data

Squire, David
    The healthy houseplants handbook
    b. Houseplants
    1. Title
    635.9'65   SB419
ISBN 0-7181-2961-X

A Marshall Edition
The Healthy Houseplants Handbook
was conceived, edited and designed by
Marshall Editions Limited, 170 Piccadilly,
London W1V 9DD

Editor   Pip Morgan
Editorial coordinator   Anne Kilborn
Art editor   Daphne Mattingly
Design assistant   Rachel Mozley
Managing editor   Ruth Binney
Production   Barry Baker

Originated by Reprocolor Llovet, SA,
Barcelona, Spain
Typeset by Vision Typesetting, Manchester, UK
Printed and bound by Usines Brepols, SA,
Turnhout, Belgium

1 2 3 4 5 92 91 90 89 88

CONTENTS

An at-a-glance identikit.
Drawings of single leaves and flowers together with simple descriptions that allow you
to identify more than 170 of the most popular
houseplants by name.

Detailed information about 82 of the most
popular houseplants.
A 'Survival Basics' feature gives details of their
requirements for light, warmth, water, food
and compost, as well as when to repot them
and their best means of propagation. Anno-
tations to the illustration of each plant indicate
problems and how to relieve them, as well as
the pests and diseases to which the plant is
particularly prone.

General advice and information about houseplant maintenance.

6

INTRODUCTION

Few homes are without houseplants. Adorning windowsills, shelves and tables are plants from the deepest jungle and the brightest desert; plants with colourful foliage or extraordinary flowers; climbing, trailing or cascading plants; shade lovers and sun worshippers. All share the need for the protection your home can provide and for treatment that matches as closely as possible the conditions prevailing in their natural habitat.

The Healthy Houseplants Handbook is concerned with helping you to keep your indoor plants alive. It is a manual for action, not for browsing. Comprehensive yet concise, practical yet attractively presented, it is above all *relevant* to the needs and demands of the amateur houseplant enthusiast.

Houseplants are rightly regarded as an essential element of an attractive modern interior. Consequently, the trade in houseplants is booming. Yet many people buy plants on impulse or simply for their looks, and then find that they lack the expertise to care adequately for their purchases. *The Healthy Houseplants Handbook* offers the information and advice

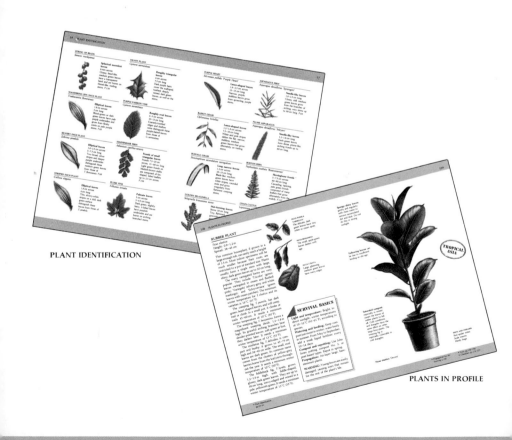

PLANT IDENTIFICATION

PLANTS IN PROFILE

they need to help their plants survive and thrive in the rigours of indoor life.

The book is divided into five clear sections. Plant Identification is a guide to help you name more than 170 of the most popular houseplants. Identification is critical since you cannot start to care for a plant properly until you know its name.

Plants in Profile describes 82 popular houseplants, including a number of their varieties and related species. The section details the needs of these houseplants, with useful survival guides that summarize the plants' basic needs. Care and Cultivation offers general advice and information on how to look after plants

(including more tricky subjects such as ferns) and how to propagate your best specimens.

Houseplant Design shows how plants can be integrated into your home or office and explains the basic concepts of using houseplants in interior design.

The ready-reference Checklist section supplies some instant answers to help decisions when shopping for houseplants and shows, at a glance, which plants are most suitable for a variety of situations.

CARE AND CULTIVATION

HOUSEPLANT DESIGN

PLANT IDENTIFICATION

This identification section is planned to enable you to identify more than 170 common houseplants, not by any complex botanical method, but by utilizing the quick and simple judgements we all make about plants, probably even without realizing it. It is an at-a-glance identikit, in which accurate, detailed drawings of single leaves or flowers are supplemented by brief texts highlighting other important features that will help identification. Plants are grouped according to their most striking common features.

USING THE IDENTIKIT

First: Check through the lists of headings below, and pick out the category your plant fits into. (Unless otherwise indicated, plants are those commonly grown for their foliage.)

- Flowering plants with an upright habit

- Flowering plants that trail or climb

- Plants that trail

- Plants that climb

- Plants with lobed leaves

- Plants with long straight leaves

- Plants with stiff tapering leaves

- Plants with patterned leaves

- Palms/Umbrella-like plants

- Plants with plantlets/Tree-like plants

Then, flick through the appropriate pages until you spot the leaf or flower that looks like yours, or close to it.

Plants that might fit into more than one of these categories are listed only once, according to what is judged to be their *outstanding* characteristic; thus the common ivy (a rampant climber) is to be found in the plants that climb section, though the shape of its leaves might have qualified it equally well for a place in the lobed leaves section.

Remember that the illustrations show the standard, most common form of each subject, so if yours is a variety, it may not match the drawing. Check further in the Plants in Profile section if you suspect you are at least on the right track.

Once you have made a visual spot check, read the accompanying text for additional clues about colour, shape, habit, texture, aroma (crush leaves if necessary), and size.

For the sake of clarity, no attempt has been made to draw plants to scale. You should note, however, that dimensions listed as 'across' refer to the width of a mature, healthy leaf at its widest point. It is also important to remember that if you have a very young plant, it may not exhibit the characteristic features of the mature specimens described: young leaves tend to be smaller, brighter and lighter in colour than older ones; they may not yet have developed lobes, nor yet adopted the typical adult growth pattern or habit.

Cross references to the Plants in Profile section (pp.32–145) guide you to fuller descriptions and detailed care instructions for many of the plants in this identikit. Any unfamiliar botanical terms are explained in the Glossary on pp.210–211.

FLOWERING PLANTS WITH AN UPRIGHT HABIT

Flowers may be large and borne singly or small and borne in dense clusters; petals may be few or many, separate or fused into a trumpet or bell-like structure. Some flowers are actually showy bracts. Prized for their individuality, plants in this section are grouped only very loosely.

CINERARIA
Senecio cruentus

Daisy-like flowers
1.8–6.5 cm across
Flowers noted for their intense colours, often offset by a circular white band. Grow in flat or domed clusters 23 cm across.
Pp.134/135

PEACE LILY
Spathiphyllum wallisii

Arum-like flowers
5 cm across
7.5 cm long
Each flower head is borne on a long stem and composed of a white, oval spathe partly enclosing an erect, cream spadix.
P.97

CHRYSANTHEMUM
Chrysanthemum spp.

Daisy-like flowers
2.5–3.5 cm across
Flowers composed of densely packed petals in a variety of forms – single, double or pompon – and colours. *Pp.58/59*

PAINTER'S PALETTE
Anthurium andreanum

Arum-like flowers
7.5 cm across
13 cm long
Each flower head is composed of a yellow spadix rising from a flattened, shiny, puckered, red spathe.
Pp.90/91

SLIPPER PLANT
Calceolaria × herbeohybrida

Pouch-like flowers
2.5–5 cm across
Loose clusters of exotic-looking blooms in yellow, orange, pink or red, often blotched or spotted in a contrasting colour.
Pp.118/119

HYDRANGEA
Hydrangea macrophylla

Large rounded flower head
15–20 cm across
10–13 cm deep
Each flower head is composed of many 4-petalled florets, each 2.5–5 cm across.
Pp.94/95

FAIRY PRIMROSE
Primula malacoides

Small circular flowers
1.2–1.8 cm across
Pink, red or white flowers, each with a yellow eye, grow in tiered whorls on long, slender stems. *P.114*

DAFFODIL
Narcissus spp.

Trumpet-shaped flowers
6–10 cm across
5–6 cm deep
Long corolla distinguishes daffodils from narcissi, which have 'cups' rather than trumpets. *Pp.38/39*

AFRICAN VIOLET
Saintpaulia ionantha

Small simple flowers
2.5–4 cm across
Purple, white, pink, blue or red flowers all have conspicuous, bright yellow pollen sacs in the centre. *Pp.82/83*

GLOXINIA
Sinningia speciosa

Large bell-shaped flowers
7.5 cm across
5–7.5 cm deep
Smooth-edged or frilled lobes at the end of a wide, deep-throated bloom in a variety of bright colours. *Pp.130/131*

PERSIAN VIOLET
Exacum affine

Small simple flowers
1.2–1.8 mm across
Profuse, fragrant, lavender-blue flowers are 5-petalled with conspicuous yellow stamens. *P.80*

ROSE OF CHINA
Hibiscus rosa-sinensis

Funnel-shaped flowers
10–13 cm across
5–6 cm deep
Fragile, papery blooms have 5 rounded petals with a prominent central column of stamens. *Pp.110/111*

HOT WATER PLANT
Achimenes longiflora

Trumpet-shaped flowers
5 cm across
4 cm deep
Narrow, tubular flowers have 5 rounded lobes. Blue or purplish-red with a white throat. *Pp.78/79*

AMARYLLIS
Hippeastrum hybrida

Large funnel-shaped flowers
13–15 cm across
7.5–10 cm deep
Tall, sturdy, straight stems bear 2–4 red, orange, white or bicoloured blooms with long stamens. *Pp.42/43*

BUSY LIZZIE
Impatiens walleriana

Flat-faced flowers
2.5–5 cm across
Long spurs project behind 5-petalled flowers borne in clusters. Single or double hybrids in pink, red, orange or multicolours. *Pp.70/71*

INDIAN AZALEA
Rhododendron simsii

Open bell-shaped flowers
5–7.5 cm across
Delicate-looking, often ruffled, petals on single or double blooms. In pink, red, white or bicolours. *Pp.74/75*

POINSETTIA
Euphorbia pulcherrima

Leaf-like bracts
Each bract 6–7.5 cm across
10–13 cm long
Spectacular, bright red bracts resemble broad, pointed leaves and surround small yellow flowers. *Pp.62/63*

COMMON HYACINTH
Hyacinthus orientalis

Spires of bell-shaped flowers
Height of spire 10–15 cm
Fragrant, waxy, 6-petalled flowers densely clustered on upright stem. In blue, red, pink, yellow or white. *Pp.34/35*

CYCLAMEN/SOW BREAD
Cyclamen persicum

Swept-back flowers
1.8–2.5 cm across
2.5–5 cm deep
Dainty flowers have 5 swept-back petals and are borne on long stalks. In pink, white, purple, red and lilac. *Pp.126/127*

SHRIMP PLANT
Justicia brandegeana

Tubular flowers
2.5–3 cm across
10–15 cm deep
Striking, overlapping, brownish-pink bracts resemble the body of a shrimp. True flowers, deep inside bracts, are small and white. *P.69*

FLAMING KATY
Kalanchoe blossfeldiana

Small tubular flowers
6 mm across
Tiny, bright red flowers with 4 pointed petals grow close together in clusters of 20–40. *P.77*

ANGEL'S TEARS
Billbergia nutans

Flower-like bracts
1.8–2.5 cm across
5–6.5 cm long
True flowers, which are green, blue and pink in colour, emerge from long, narrow, pink bracts borne in drooping clusters. *P.41*

CHENILLE PLANT
Acalypha hispida

Tassle-like flowers
Tassle 1.8–2.5 cm across
20–30 cm long
Unusual, drooping, bright scarlet spikes composed of many small flowers resemble silken embroidery tassles. Also in green or cream. *P.73*

FLOWERING PLANTS THAT TRAIL OR CLIMB

Many of these common houseplants bear rather exotic, unfamiliar-looking flowers. As well as observing their structure, note how they are borne — whether in clusters or singly, at the end of, or along, the length of their generally fragile stems. Remember that young plants may not yet have started to trail or climb.

FUCHSIA
Fuchsia spp.

Pendulous bell-shaped flowers
1.8—4 cm across
2.5—5 cm deep
Flowers have long stamens and a longer style protruding from corolla which contrasts in colour with the 4 arching sepals.

RAT'S TAIL CACTUS
Aporocactus flagelliformis

Tubular flowers
5 cm across
5—7.5 cm long
Bright pink or magenta flowers have many overlapping, pointed, outward-curving petals and prominent yellow stamens. *Pp.138/139*

GOLDFISH PLANT
Columnea × banksii

Tubular hooded flowers
4 cm across
6—7.5 cm long
Vermilion flowers have orange-yellow lines in the throat. Two lobes of the corolla form a 'hood'. *P.66*

EASTER CACTUS
Rhipsalidopsis gaertneri

Tubular flowers
4—6 cm across
4—5 cm long
Many bright red, pointed petals overlap in a roughly tubular shape. Pendulous flowers appear at ends of branching segments. *Pp.142/143*

GOLDFISH PLANT
Columnea gloriosa

Tubular hooded flowers
4 cm across
5—6 cm long
Distinguished from *C. × banksii* by soft, white down on the scarlet corolla and yellow patch on the throat. *Pp.66/67*

CRAB CACTUS
Schlumbergera truncata

Tubular flowers
5 cm across
5—7.5 cm long
Slender, elegant, pink to deep red flowers with numerous turned-back petals contrast with 'crab-claw' stems. *P.142*

FIRECRACKER PLANT
Manettia inflata

Tubular flowers
6 mm across
1.8 cm long
Reddish, hairy flowers are tipped in yellow and have a green calyx divided into 5 arched, petal-like sections.

13

SPANISH SHAWL
Schizocentron elegans

Simple flowers
2.5 cm across
Rose-purple flowers, borne individually at stem tips, are 4-petalled and have conspicuous, central clusters of arching, purple stamens.

PINK JASMINE
Jasminum polyanthum

Star-shaped tubular flowers
2.5 cm across
2.5–3 cm long
A climber with 5-petalled, fragrant, pale pink flowers borne in clusters near ends of stems. *P.117*

CAPE LEADWORT
Plumbago auriculata

Star-faced tubular flowers
2.5 cm across
2.5–3 cm long
Flowers composed of long, narrow tube flaring into open arrangement of 5 pale blue petals, each with a dark blue line.

PRIMROSE JASMINE
Jasminum mesnyi

Star-shaped tubular flowers
2.5 cm across
1.8 cm long
Semi-double, non-fragrant, yellow flowers have dark centres. Tubes are shorter than those of *J. polyanthum.*

IVY-LEAVED PELARGONIUM
Pelargonium peltatum

Star-shaped flowers
2.5 cm across
Carmine-pink, red or white flowers, composed of 5 petals (2 pointing up, 3 down), are borne in small clusters on stalks 15–23 cm long. *P.102*

MADAGASCAR JASMINE
Stephanotis floribunda

Star-shaped tubular flowers
2.5 cm across
4 cm long
A climber with fragrant, waxy, white flowers that have 5 pointed lobes flaring from narrow tube and are borne in clusters.

BASKET BEGONIA
Begonia × tuberhybrida 'Pendula'

Rose-like flowers
5–7.5 cm across
Trailing form with large, many-petalled blooms available in pink, red, yellow and white. *P.122*

MINIATURE WAX FLOWER
Hoya bella

Star-shaped tubular flowers
Clusters 5 cm across
4 cm deep
Fragrant, waxy, white flowers have red-purple centres. Borne in clusters of up to 10 on climbing stems.

PLANTS THAT TRAIL

Rather than a strong, upright central stem these plants tend to produce several thin, rather unsubstantial stems. Some have a natural and unalterable propensity to trail; others, will grow upright with support. In the case of some succulents, the weight of the foliage dictates the trailing habit.

SWEDISH IVY

Plectranthus australis

Heart-shaped leaves
1.8–2.5 cm across
2.5–4 cm long
Dark green, waxy leaves have scalloped edges and prominent, rib-like veins. Plant is bushy, then sprawling.

CREEPING FIG

Ficus pumila

Heart-shaped leaves
2.5 cm across
2.5 cm long
Prominently-veined, dark green leaves are borne on wiry stems that creep, trail or climb. *P.108*

SWEETHEART PLANT

Philodendron scandens

Heart-shaped leaves
7.5 cm across
10 cm long
Pointed, shiny, medium green leaves have a bronze transparency when young. With age, they become darker and more pointed. *P.101*

SWEDISH IVY

Plectranthus oertendahlii

Heart-shaped leaves
2.5 cm across
2.5–3 cm long
Broad, green leaves have prominent silvery-white veins that turn rosy-purple with age.

DEVIL'S IVY

Epipremnum pinnatum 'Aureum'

Heart-shaped leaves
4–5 cm across
10–15 cm long
Bright yellow markings on dark green, shiny, pointed leaves that are alternately arranged. Young leaves oval and dark green. *P.100*

CANDLE FLOWER

Plectranthus coleoides 'Marginatus'

Heart-shaped leaves
4 cm across
5–6 cm long
Pale green leaves have creamy-white, scalloped edges. Plant is upright at first, then trails.

CUPID PEPEROMIA

Peperomia scandens

Heart-shaped leaves
4 cm across
5 cm long
Glossy, medium green leaves. *P. s.* 'Variegata' is mostly yellow when young, then turns green with cream edges.

BABY'S TEARS / MIND YOUR OWN BUSINESS
Soleirolia soleirolii

Circular to heart-shaped leaves
5 mm across
Tiny, glossy, pale to medium green leaves grow on pinkish stalks. Plant bushy, then trailing and spreading.

MOTHER OF THOUSANDS
Saxifraga stolonifera 'Tricolor'

Circular to heart-shaped leaves
7.5 cm across
Pink, white and green leaves have red undersides. Red, trailing runners up to 90 cm long develop plantlets at their ends.

BUTTON FERN
Pellaea rotundifolia

Circular to heart-shaped leaves
1.2 cm across
Shiny, button-like, dark green leaves borne alternately on dark, wiry, cascading stems. *P.65*

PAINTED NET LEAF / MOSAIC PLANT
Fittonia verschaffeltii

Round to oval leaves
5–6 cm across
7.5–13 cm long
Distinctive network of deep pink veins covers thick, dark green leaves. *P.76*

STRING OF HEARTS
Ceropegia woodii

Circular to heart-shaped leaves
1.8 cm across
Fleshy, dark green leaves, marbled in silver, are borne sparsely on purplish, thread-like, trailing stems.

VARIEGATED GROUND IVY
Glechoma hederacea variegata

Kidney-shaped leaves
2.5 cm across
1.8–2.5 cm long
Pale to medium green leaves have white, scalloped and toothed edges.

JAPANESE SEDUM
Sedum seiboldii

Circular to heart-shaped leaves
1.8 cm across
Succulent, flat, grey leaves have pink, notched edges and are borne in threes around cascading stems.

BURRO'S TAIL
Sedum morganianum

Rounded succulent leaves
1 cm thick
2 cm long
Pointed, grey-green, fleshy leaves overlap to form dense, trailing, tail-like stems, 60–90 cm long. *P.144*

STRING OF BEADS
Senecio rowleyanus

Spherical succulent leaves
6 mm across
Glossy, bead-like, medium green leaves have a transparent band and are borne on thread-like, trailing stems. *P.134*

VELVET PLANT
Gynura sarmentosa

Roughly triangular leaves
4 cm across
7.5 cm long
Dark purple hairs cover the scalloped, toothed, deeply veined, dark green leaves, as well as the stems.

WANDERING JEW/INCH PLANT
Tradescantia fluminensis

Elliptical leaves
1.8 cm across
5 cm long
Bluish-green or dark green leaves have pale purple undersides and grow from fleshy joints on pale purple stems. *P.68*

PURPLE PASSION VINE
Gynura aurantiaca

Roughly oval leaves
4–5 cm across
10–13 cm long
Coarsely-toothed edges and shallow veins distinguish these purple-haired leaves from those of *G. sarmentosa.*

SILVERY INCH PLANT
Zebrina pendula

Elliptical leaves
1.8–2.5 cm across
5–7.5 cm long
Two broad, silver stripes and deeper purple undersides distinguish these medium green leaves from those of *T. fluminensis. P.68*

MAIDENHAIR FERN
Adiantum capillus-veneris

Fronds of small triangular leaves
Fronds 7.5–25 cm across, 15–60 cm long
Light green fronds on blackish-brown stalks are composed of fan-shaped, lobed leaflets up to 2.5 cm across. *P.136*

STRIPED INCH PLANT
Callisia elegans

Elliptical leaves
1.8 cm across
4 cm long
Thin, silvery-white stripes on a dull, dark green surface distinguish these leaves from those of *Z. pendula.*

PLUSH VINE
Mikania ternata

Palmate leaves
5 cm across
5–6.5 cm long
Dark green, slightly hairy, 3-lobed leaves have purplish undersides and are borne on arching, branched stems.

PURPLE HEART
Setcreasea pallida 'Purple Heart'

Lance-shaped leaves
1.8–2.5 cm across
13–15 cm long
Narrow, purple,
stalkless leaves grow
from sprawling, purple
stems.

ASPARAGUS FERN
Asparagus densiflorus 'Sprengeri'

Needle-like leaves
1.8–2.5 cm long
Glossy, stiff, medium
green leaves grow
from the branches of
arching, wiry stems up
to 90 cm long. *P.64*

BASKET GRASS
Oplismenus hirtellus

Lance-shaped leaves
1.2–1.8 cm across
7.5–10 cm long
White and pink stripes
define the flat, narrow,
stalkless, medium
green leaves that grow
alternately on trailing
stems.

PLUME ASPARAGUS
Asparagus densiflorus 'Meyeri'

Needle-like leaves
1.2–1.8 cm long
Fresh green leaves
form dense, plume-like,
arching fronds up to
60 cm long.

BUFFALO GRASS
Stenotaphrum secundatum variegatum

Long narrow leaves
1.2 cm across
10–15 cm long
Blade-like, medium
green leaves have
white stripes, rounded
ends and grow
irregularly from
flattened, creeping
stems.

BOSTON FERN
Nephrolepis exaltata 'Bostoniensis'

Herringbone fronds
5–7.5 cm across
60–90 cm long
Cascading, tapering,
pale green fronds
composed of many
leaflets that grow
alternately from the
midrib. *P.137*

GOLDEN SELAGINELLA
Selaginella kraussiana aurea

Mat-forming leaves
Stems 30 cm long
Tiny, flattened,
greenish-yellow leaves
grow in overlapping
ranks around creeping
stems.

CHAIN CACTUS
Lepismium paradoxum

Chain-like stems
1.2–1.8 cm across
5–7.5 cm long
Flattened, medium to
light green stems are
segmented and
irregularly branched.

PLANTS THAT CLIMB

Though plants may have a natural tendency to climb, they will not do so indoors without support. Some will use thin tendrils to cling to the support you provide; those without tendrils will need tying with wire or twine. Without support, these plants will trail, and, indeed, some are commonly cultivated as trailers.

ELEPHANT'S EAR
Philodendron domesticum

Spear-shaped leaves
6 cm across
18 cm long
Glossy, elongated, smooth-edged, medium green leaves are borne on thick, fleshy stalks. *P.101*

BLACK GOLD
Philodendron melanochrysum

Heart-shaped leaves
7.5–10 cm across
15–60 cm long
Prominent, ivory veins highlight the velvety, dark green leaves that have purple undersides. With age, they become elongated. *P.101*

BLUSHING PHILODENDRON
Philodendron erubescens

Arrow-shaped leaves
6–7.5 cm across
23 cm long
A coppery tinge to the glossy, dark green leaves, and the purple-tinged stalks, distinguish this from *P. domesticum*. *P.101*

KANGAROO VINE
Cissus antarctica

Heart-shaped leaves
5 cm across
10 cm long
Toothed, pointed, glossy, dark green leaves grow singly from short, red stalks. *P.61*

ARROWHEAD VINE / GOOSEFOOT VINE
Syngonium podophyllum

Arrow-shaped leaves
5–6 cm across
7.5–13 cm long
Medium green leaves change dramatically in shape as they mature, and earlike lobes divide into as many as 8 separate leaflets. *P.116*

ORNAMENTAL PEPPER
Piper crocatum

Heart-shaped leaves
5–6 cm across
7.5–13 cm long
Puckered, pointed, bronze-green leaves are flecked with pink, have red undersides and grow on short, red stalks.

BEGONIA VINE
Cissus discolor

Pointed heart-shaped leaves
5–6 cm across
10–15 cm long
Silver and pale purple markings between the sunken, green veins contrast with maroon-red undersides. *P.61*

19

CAPE IVY

Senecio macroglossus

3-lobed leaves
6 cm across
6 cm long
Roughly triangular,
waxy, fleshy, dark
green leaves.
Variegated form has
golden-yellow
blotches.

NEEDLEPOINT IVY

Hedera helix 'Sagittaefolia'

5-lobed leaves
5–7.5 cm across
7.5–8 cm long
Central lobe of the
arrow-shaped, glossy,
dark green leaves is
markedly longer than
the others. *P.113*

GERMAN IVY

Senecio mikanioides

5–7-lobed leaves
5–6 cm across
5–6 cm long
Pointed lobes and
sunken veins
distinguish the fleshy,
dark green leaves.
Variegated form has
yellow blotches. *P.134*

COMMON IVY

Hedera helix

3–5 lobed leaves
5–7.5 cm across
5–7.5 cm long
Leaves may be all-
green or variegated
with yellow, white,
grey or blue-green.
Lobes may be round,
pointed or crinkled.
P.113

CANARY ISLAND IVY

Hedera canariensis 'Variegata'

3-lobed leaves
6–8 cm across
6–8 cm long
Yellow-white edges
and silver markings
typify the slightly
heart-shaped, dark
green leaves. Stems
and stalks are red.

MERMAID VINE

Cissus rhombifolia 'Ellen Danica'

**Diamond-shaped
leaves**
4–5 cm across
5 cm long
Leaf distinguished
from that of
C. rhombifolia by its
near-circular shape and
deeply scalloped
edges.

GOLDENHEART IVY

Hedera helix 'Jubilee'

3-lobed leaves
5–6 cm across
6 cm long
Centre of the leathery,
dark green leaves is
variegated golden-
yellow. *P.113*

GRAPE IVY

Cissus rhombifolia

**Diamond-shaped
leaves**
10–13 cm across
10–13 cm long
Glossy, dark green
leaves are scalloped,
spiny-edged and
arranged in threes.
Young leaves are
silvery green. *P.61*

PLANTS WITH LOBED LEAVES

A slight tendency toward lobing is evident in many leaves. Those shown here have pronounced indentations or incisions that produce distinct, though never separate, segments. These lobes vary in number not only between different species but even between leaves on the same plant. The degree of lobing may increase or decrease with age.

IVY-LEAVED PELARGONIUM

Pelargonium peltatum

3–5-lobed leaves
5–7.5 cm across
5–6 cm long
Ivy-like, fleshy, shiny, medium green leaves grow on brittle, trailing stems. *P.102*

LEMON-SCENTED GERANIUM

Pelargonium crispum

3-lobed leaves
4–5 cm across
4–5 cm long
Crinkled, tooth-edged, medium green leaves have unmistakable lemon fragrance. *P.102*

IVY TREE

× *Fatshedera lizei*

5-lobed leaves
13 cm across
21 cm long
Shiny, leathery, dark green leaves with deep central veins and long stalks grow densely on thin, erect stems. Older plants sprawl. *P.124*

PEPPERMINT GERANIUM

Pelargonium tomentosum

3-lobed leaves
4–7.5 cm across
4–7.5 cm long
Velvety, shallowly lobed, pale green leaves have a distinct mint fragrance.

CASTOR OIL PLANT

Ricinus communis

5–7-lobed leaves
18–23 cm across
15–20 cm long
Ribbed, serrated, medium green leaves are more deeply lobed than *Fatsia japonica* and turn reddish when mature.

SPOTTED FLOWERING MAPLE

Abutilon striatum 'Thompsonii'

3–5-lobed leaves
10–13 cm across
8–10 cm long
Dark green leaves are mottled yellow, stems are woody and flowers are bell-shaped, orange and veined in crimson.

FALSE CASTOR OIL PLANT

Fatsia japonica

7–9-lobed leaves
20–25 cm across
18–23 cm long
Deeply indented leaves have pointed, medium green, finger-like lobes with serrated edges.

BEGONIA
Begonia 'Cleopatra'

7-lobed leaves
5–6 cm across
5–6 cm long
Bronze-green leaves
have chocolate edges
and white hairs
underneath. Plant is
small, bushy and
multistemmed.

LACY TREE PHILODENDRON
Philodendron selloum

Multilobed leaves
30 cm across
30–45 cm long
Deep green, leathery
leaves grow on stiff
stalks and form a
rosette. Smaller, less
incised than
P. bipinnatifidum.

ROSE GERANIUM
Pelargonium capitatum

7-lobed leaves
4–5 cm across
5 cm long
Soft, light green leaves
are slightly toothed,
grow on trailing stems
and have a rose-like
fragrance.

STAG'S HORN FERN
Platycerium bifurcatum

Multilobed fronds
15–20 cm across
60–90 cm long
Stiff, leathery, fertile
fronds are smoothly
and deeply indented
and resemble the
antlers of a stag.

ROSE GERANIUM
Pelargonium graveolens

7–9-lobed leaves
6–7.5 cm across
6–7.5 cm long
Grey-green, aromatic
leaves are more deeply
lobed and more
sharply toothed than
P. capitatum.

SWISS CHEESE PLANT
Monstera deliciosa

Incised perforated leaves
45–60 cm across
60–75 cm long
Shiny, dark green
leaves have deep
slashes and holes.
Young leaves heart-
shaped without
incisions. *P.105*

TREE PHILODENDRON
Philodendron bipinnatifidum

Multilobed leaves
30–45 cm across
45–60 cm long
Deep incisions divide
the mature, arrow-
shaped leaves into
many fingers, but
young leaves are
heart-shaped without
incisions.

CROTON/JOSEPH'S COAT
Codiaeum variegatum 'Disraeli'

Deeply lobed leaves
4–7.5 cm across
10–15 cm long
Leathery, medium
green leaves are 3-
lobed, mottled yellow
and flushed dark red
underneath. *P.54*

PLANTS WITH LONG STRAIGHT LEAVES

These leaves are often borne in arching, rosette-like clusters. Some are broad and 'strap-like' (of a constant width for most of their length), others are narrower and taper gradually along their length like the blade of a sword. Edges are often finely toothed or serrated.

CORAL BERRY
Aechmea fulgens discolor

Stiff strap-like leaves
6–7.5 cm across
25–30 cm long
Saw-edged, leathery, olive-green leaves have reddish-purple undersides covered with white powder.
P.46

BLUSHING BROMELIAD
Neoregelia carolinae 'Tricolor'

Stiff strap-like leaves
2.5–3 cm across
20–30 cm long
Cream and rose-pink stripes distinguish the saw-edged, glossy, arching, green leaves.
Pp.50/51

AMAZONIAN ZEBRA PLANT
Aechmea chantinii

Stiff strap-like leaves
5 cm across
25–30 cm long
Silvery-white scales form regular cross-bands on both sides of the dark green leaves.
P.46

FINGERNAIL PLANT
Neoregelia spectabilis

Stiff strap-like leaves
2.5–3 cm across
30 cm long
A bright red spot highlights the tip of each leathery, metallic-green leaf. *P.50*

VRIESEA
Vriesea fenestralis

Stiff strap-like leaves
2.5–4 cm across
30–38 cm long
Fine, dark green stripes distinguish the arching, light green leaves. Undersides are finely striped in purple.

URN PLANT
Aechmea fasciata

Stiff strap-like leaves
6–7.5 cm across
20–30 cm long
Silvery scales form irregular bands or mottling on thick, saw-edged, arching, grey-green leaves.
Pp.46/47

KING OF BROMELIADS
Vriesea hieroglyphica

Stiff strap-like leaves
6–7.5 cm across
38–45 cm long
Irregular, purple cross-bands distinguish the erect then arching, yellow-green leaves.

FLAMING SWORD
Vriesea splendens

Stiff strap-like leaves
4–5 cm across
38 cm long
Regular, dark purple
cross-bands distinguish
the erect then arching,
dark green leaves. *P.40*

SCREW PINE
Pandanus veitchii

**Long sword-like
leaves**
2.5–4 cm across
60–90 cm long
Spiny-edged, shiny,
green leaves are
striped and edged in
cream. Mature, arched
leaves are spirally
arranged. *P.36*

STRIPED TORCH
Guzmania monostachya

Stiff strap-like leaves
18 cm across
30–38 cm long
Narrow, pale green
leaves are erect then
slightly arched. *P.48*

DRAGON TREE
Dracaena deremensis 'Warneckii'

Spear-shaped leaves
1.8–3 cm across
38 cm long
Narrow, arching,
stalkless, green leaves
rise from a central
stem and have two
white stripes. *P.96*

SCARLET STAR
Guzmania lingulata

Stiff strap-like leaves
2.5 cm across
30–38 cm long
Shiny, metallic-green
leaves are wider and
more arched than
those of
G. monostachya. P.48

TI LOG PLANT
Cordyline fruticosa

Spear-shaped leaves
2.5–4 cm across
25–30 cm long
Sharply-tapering leaves
are light crimson when
young. They become
bronze-green and
shaded red with age.
Pp.98/99

PINEAPPLE PLANT
Ananas comosus

**Long stiff sword-
like leaves**
4 cm across
45 cm long
Leaves are spiny-
edged, upward-arching
and grey-green.
A. c. variegatus has
broad, ivory and pink
margins. *P.52*

CAST IRON PLANT
Aspidistra elatior

Spear-shaped leaves
7.5–10 cm across
23–38 cm long
Arching, bright green
leaves grow on short,
stiff, upright stalks.
They blacken with
age. *P.93*

PLANTS WITH STIFF TAPERING LEAVES

Often tough or even fleshy, these leaves tend to be rather more squat and solid in appearance than those included in the previous section. Most grow in dense rosettes and some are armed with sharp, pointed ends or sharply spined edges.

EARTH STAR
Cryptanthus fosterianus

Wavy spiny-edged leaves
3–3.5 cm across
30–38 cm long
Dark copper-brown colour of the grey-banded leaves distinguishes them from those of *C. zonatus*.

EARTH STAR
Cryptanthus bivittatus

Wavy spiny-edged leaves
1.8–2.5 cm across
7.5–10 cm long
A rosy tinge colours the light and dark green stripes on the stiff, tapering leaves. *P.45*

RAINBOW STAR
Cryptanthus bromelioides 'Tricolor'

Wavy spiny-edged leaves
3–3.5 cm across
18–20 cm long
Upright rosette of green leaves with creamy-white stripes tinged pink, and white scaly undersides.

STARFISH PLANT
Cryptanthus acaulis

Wavy spiny-edged leaves
3 cm across
10–13 cm long
Pale green colour and grey, scaly undersides distinguish the leaves from those of *C. bivittatus*. *P.45*

MOTHER-IN-LAW'S TONGUE
Sansevieria trifasciata 'Laurentii'

Stiff lance-shaped leaves
5–7.5 cm across
38–45 cm long
Smooth, creamy-yellow edges and irregular, grey cross-bands highlight the erect, dark green leaves. *P.53*

EARTH STAR
Cryptanthus zonatus

Wavy spiny-edged leaves
3–3.5 cm across
15–20 cm long
Irregular, grey cross-bands and grey-white undersides distinguish the large, grass-green leaves.

BIRD'S NEST SANSEVIERIA
Sansevieria trifasciata 'Hahnii'

Elliptical leaves
5 cm across
13–15 cm long
Shiny, pointed, deep green leaves have irregular, grey cross-bands and form a squat rosette. *P.53*

SPINELESS YUCCA
Yucca elephantipes

Strap-like leaves
5—7.5 cm across
75—90 cm long
Glossy, pointed, dark
green leaves are soft-
tipped, rough-edged
and form rosettes
which arch outward at
the top of a thick
stem. *P.49*

QUEEN AGAVE
Agave victoriae-reginae

Triangular leaves
2.5—3 cm across
10—13 cm long
White edges and
stripes distinguish the
dark green leaves that
have black-spined tips
and form a spherical
rosette.

SPANISH BAYONET
Yucca aloifolia

Strap-like leaves
5—6 cm across
45—75 cm long
Serrated edges and
sharp, pointed tips
distinguish the stiff,
dark green leaves from
those of *Y. elephantipes.*
P.49

PARTRIDGE-BREASTED ALOE
Aloe variegata

Triangular leaves
4—5 cm across
7.5—13 cm long
Irregular, white cross-
bands and white edges
highlight the tooth-
edged, pointed, dark
grey-green leaves. *P.44*

CENTURY PLANT
Agave americana 'Marginata'

Sword-shaped leaves
6—7.5 cm across
30—45 cm long
Golden-yellow edges
highlight the thick,
fleshy, spiny-edged,
grey-green leaves
which form a rosette.

CROTON
Codiaeum variegatum pictum

**Variously shaped
leaves**
4—7.5 cm across
10—15 cm long
Leaf shown is one of
the many possible
shapes; others may be
longer, narrower or
lobed. All are
multicoloured. *Pp.54/55*

THREAD AGAVE
Agave filifera

Sword-shaped leaves
2.5—4 cm across
20—30 cm long
Fine, white threads
edge the medium
green leaves that turn
upward and form a
rosette.

BIRD'S NEST FERN
Asplenium nidus

Strap-like fronds
7.5—13 cm across
30—60 cm long
Glossy, wavy-edged,
apple-green fronds rise
in a loose rosette. Each
frond has a brown
midrib. *P.141*

PLANTS WITH PATTERNED LEAVES

Stripes, spots, speckles, blotches – sometimes random, sometimes regular, and often combined with prominent, brightly coloured veins – distinguish many leaves. These variegations are most commonly in silver, creamy-yellow, or white, but in some cases brilliant, deeper hues produce the characteristic effect.

CALATHEA
Calathea ornata

Oval to spear-shaped leaves
5–6 cm across
15–18 cm long
Thin, rosy stripes fading to ivory or white distinguish the dark green leaves. Coloured purple-red underneath.

RABBIT TRACKS
Maranta leuconeura kerchoveana

Oblong leaves
5–6 cm across
6–7.5 cm long
Brown markings resembling a rabbit's footprints appear on each side of the midrib of light green leaves. *P.86*

ALUMINIUM PLANT
Pilea cadierei

Oval to round leaves
4–5 cm across
5–7.5 cm long
Leathery, rough-edged, dark green leaves have raised, silvery splashes between the veins. *P.72*

HERRINGBONE PLANT
Maranta leuconeura erythrophylla

Oblong leaves
5–6 cm across
6–7.5 cm long
Red veins and jagged, light green markings along the midrib highlight the olive-green leaves. *Pp.86/87*

RATTLESNAKE PLANT
Calathea insignis

Lance-shaped leaves
4–5 cm across
13–15 cm long
Wavy, pale green leaves have alternate, large and small, dark green blotches beside the midrib. Maroon underneath. *P.88*

PEACOCK PLANT
Calathea makoyana

Oval to spear-shaped leaves
6–7.5 cm across
10–15 cm long
Silvery-green leaves have dark, oval markings linked to medium green edges by fine lines. *P.88*

ZEBRA PLANT
Calathea zebrina

Elliptical leaves
5–6 cm across
20–45 cm long
Horizontally-held, emerald-green leaves are distinguished by regular, bright green bands between the veins. *P.88*

BOAT LILY
Rhoeo spathacea

Sword-shaped leaves
4–5 cm across
20–30 cm long
Upright, tapering, dark green leaves have rich purple undersides and form a loose rosette on a short, thick stem. *P.37*

POLKA DOT PLANT
Hypoestes phyllostachya

Pointed oval leaves
4–5 cm across
5 cm long
Olive-green leaves grow in pairs on upright stems and are covered in rosy-pink spots and splashes. *P.81*

DUMB CANE
Dieffenbachia maculata 'Exotica'

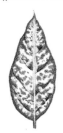

Spear-shaped leaves
5–7.5 cm across
20–30 cm long
Glossy, green leaves are liberally splashed in pale creamy-yellow, with pale green edges. *P.89*

IRON CROSS BEGONIA
Begonia masoniana

Obliquely heart-shaped leaves
15 cm across
13–15 cm long
Puckered, medium green leaves are distinguished by a central 'cross' with 4–5 bronze-purple 'arms'. *Pp.120/121*

ZEBRA PLANT
Aphelandra squarrosa

Spear-shaped leaves
5–10 cm across
18–23 cm long
Glossy, dark green leaves have bold, ivory-coloured veins and midrib. Plant produces showy, yellow bracts. *Pp.106/107*

SILVER LACE FERN
Pteris ensiformis 'Victoriae'

Triangular fronds
10–13 cm across
20–25 cm long
Unevenly arranged, finger-like, deep green leaflets make up the fronds. They are highlighted by silvery-white centres. Leaflets branch with age. *P.140*

CHINESE EVERGREEN
Aglaonema treubii

Spear-shaped leaves
5–6 cm across
15–23 cm long
Pointed, glossy, leathery, grey-green leaves have silvery-grey splashes. *P.92*

EMERALD RIPPLE
Peperomia caperata

Heart-shaped leaves
1.8–2.5 cm across
3 cm long
Glistening, dark green leaves have purple-tinged corrugations and grow on pink stalks. *P.84*

PALMS / UMBRELLA-LIKE PLANTS

Palms are perceived as fronds – groups of leaflets radiating from a cental stem or borne like a fan at the end of a leaf stalk. Similarly, umbrella-like leaf arrangements must be viewed in their entirety. The characteristic arrangement of a number of leaves or leaflets typifies the plants in this section.

CANARY DATE PALM

Phoenix canariensis

Fronds with leaflets on either side of midrib
25–30 cm across
75–90 cm long
Stiff, spiky, dark green leaflets are regularly and evenly paired. Indoors, fronds soften with age. *P.133*

KENTIA PALM

Howeia forsteriana

Fronds with leaflets on either side of midrib
30 cm across
45–60 cm long
Arching, dark green leaflets are held horizontally and spaced 2.5 cm apart. *P.129*

PYGMY DATE PALM

Phoenix roebelenii

Fronds with leaflets on either side of midrib
25 cm across
45–60 cm long
Arching fronds form a thick crown and are composed of thin, arching, dark green leaflets. *P.133*

SENTRY PALM

Howeia belmoreana

Fronds with leaflets on either side of midrib
30 cm across
45 cm long
Leaflets are narrower and closer than those of *H. forsteriana* and are held almost vertically. *P.129*

DWARF COCONUT PALM

Microcoelum weddeliana

Fronds with leaflets on either side of midrib
20–25 cm across
30–38 cm long
Narrow, arching, dark green leaflets are evenly arranged around a black-scaled midrib.

PARLOUR PALM

Chamaedorea elegans

Fronds with leaflets on either side of midrib
20–25 cm across
25–38 cm long
Arching, lance-shaped, deep green leaflets are almost paired along the length of the stalk. *P.132*

SAGO PALM

Cycas revoluta

Feather-like fronds
15–20 cm across
38–45 cm long
Fronds grow from pineapple-shaped base and have tightly-packed, dark green leaflets.

EUROPEAN FAN PALM
Chamaerops humilis

Fronds with leaflets at tips of stems
38–38 cm across
15–20 cm long
Stiff, fan-like fronds grow from toothed stems and have green, sword-like leaflets.

UMBRELLA PLANT
Cyperus alternifolius

Umbrella-like bract arrangement
15–30 cm across
Arching, narrow, pale green bracts are leaf-like and grow on rush-like stems. *P.56*

LITTLE LADY PALM
Rhapis excelsa

Fronds with leaflets at tips of stems
25–30 cm across
15–20 cm long
Fronds grow from clustered stems and have 5–8 stiff, segmented, dark green leaflets.

UMBRELLA PLANT
Cyperus diffusus

Umbrella-like bract arrangement
15–25 cm across
Leaf-like bracts are wider and darker than those of *C. alternifolius*. *P.56*

ARECA PALM
Chrysalidocarpus lutescens

Fronds with cane-like stems
30–45 cm across
45–60 cm long
Arching fronds grow on clustered stems and have stiff, arching, alternately-arranged, yellow-green leaflets.

REED PALM
Chamaedorea seifrizii

Fronds with cane-like stems
38–60 cm across
38–60 cm long
Fronds more delicate than those of the areca palm; leaflets are narrower and a deeper green.

FALSE ARALIA
Dizygotheca elegantissima

Umbrella-like leaf arrangement
10–13 cm across
Leathery, saw-edged leaves are coppery-red, turning dark green with age. *P.57*

BAMBOO PALM
Chamaedorea erumpens

Fronds with cane-like stems
38–55 cm across
38–55 cm long
Arching fronds have broad, widely-spaced, deep green leaflets; the last pair are broader than the rest.

PLANTS WITH PLANTLETS/ TREE-LIKE PLANTS

A feature of some plants is the way they reproduce small replicas of themselves. They may be borne on the end of runners or from the edges of mature leaves. Tree-like plants have an impressive upright habit, often with a woody, central stem. Many grow into trees in the wild.

MEXICAN HAT PLANT
Kalanchoe daigremontiana

Leaves with plantlets
4–5 cm across
7.5–10 cm long
Plantlets grow at edges of toothed, triangular, succulent, pale green leaves. *P.77*

PIGGY-BACK PLANT
Tolmiea menziesii

Leaves with plantlets
5 cm across
5–6 cm long
Plantlets grow from top surface of mature, heart-shaped, downy leaves at junction with stalk. *P.112*

SPIDER PLANT/ST. BERNARD'S LILY
Chlorophytum comosum

Plantlets on runners
Plantlets borne on stiff, arching, white stems which emerge from green, cream-striped leaves, 1.2–1.8 cm wide and 20–25 cm long. *P.60*

HEN AND CHICKEN FERN
Asplenium bulbiferum

Fronds with plantlets
20–25 cm across
45–60 cm long
Plantlets grow at edges of mature, feathery, upright then arching, medium green fronds. *P.141*

RUBBER PLANT
Ficus elastica

Oblong to oval leaves
7.5–10 cm across
20–30 cm long
Erect, unbranched plant has stiff, glossy, dark green leaves with prominent midribs. *Pp.108/109*

CHANDELIER PLANT
Kalanchoe tubiflora

Leaves with plantlets
6 mm across
5–13 cm long
Plantlets grow singly or in clusters at the ends of tubular, succulent, medium green leaves with red-brown markings.

WEEPING FIG
Ficus benjamina

Elliptical leaves
2.5–4 cm across
7.5–10 cm long
Stiff, pale green leaves darken with age. They droop gracefully from arching branches. *P.108*

FIDDLEBACK FIG
Ficus lyrata

Fiddle-shaped leaves
10–13 cm across
30–38 cm long
Erect plant has glossy, wavy-edged, waxy, dark green leaves with prominent yellow-green veins. *P.108*

UMBRELLA TREE
Brassaia actinophylla

Umbrella-like leaf arrangement
15–23 cm across
Similar to *S. arboricola*. Oval, olive-green leaves are 4–5 in number, leathery, glossy, and up to 30 cm long. *P.104*

BENGAL FIG / BANYAN TREE
Ficus benghalensis

Oval leaves
7.5–10 cm across
20 cm long
Many-branched plant has leathery, dark green leaves with yellow-green veins. Leaves and stem are covered with fine, reddish-brown hairs.

NORFOLK ISLAND PINE
Araucaria heterophylla

Tiered branches
20–25 cm across
30–45 cm long
Tiered branches on erect, woody stem are densely covered with short needles that are bright green when young, darkening with age. *P.128*

SILK OAK
Grevillea robusta

Fern-like fronds
15–20 cm across
30–45 cm long
Upper surfaces of mature, deep green fronds of erect plant are downy; undersides covered in silky hairs. *P.145*

FERN TREE
Jacaranda mimosifolia

Fern-like fronds
10–15 cm across
30–38 cm long
Single-stemmed at first, then branching. Bright green leaves are composed of about 20 pairs of leaflets.

PARASOL PLANT
Schefflera arboricola

Umbrella-like leaf arrangement
15–23 cm across
Branching stalks, 22–30 cm long, of erect plant end in at least 7, narrow, pointed, glossy, green leaves, each on a 2.5 cm stalk. P.104

CORAL BERRY
Ardisia crenata

Lance-shaped leaves
4–5 cm across
10 cm long
Upright shrub has leathery, shiny, wavy-edged, deep green leaves. Clusters of small, white flowers are followed by bright red berries. *P.85*

PLANTS IN PROFILE

More than 80 of the most popular plants grown indoors are 'profiled' in this section. Colour illustrations capture the brilliance of many flowering subjects; others are shown in plain green, though this does not in any way approximate to the vibrant natural greens of the leaves in question.

Each profile opens with a detailed description of the leaves, flowers and habits of the plant featured. The 'stamps' on each page indicate the plant's place of origin. The stamp that reads HYBRID means that the plant has been created by man and not by nature.

Where interesting varieties are available, offering other colours, sizes, shapes and habits, they are also indicated. Details are given of further recommended species of the same genus as well as of plants with distinct similarities to the one featured. In the headings, common names are followed by the currently accepted Latin name. Readers may, in some cases, be more familiar with synonyms now officially superseded. These are given, where necessary, in the text.

The approximate height and spread of a mature specimen reared under the recommended conditions is indicated below the heading. Some plants would, naturally, grow larger in a warm greenhouse or in a large container placed in a conservatory.

Many houseplants are actually extremely resilient, but if you follow the practical advice in the Survival Basics box accompanying each plant you will ensure that your plants will not only survive but flourish. All the data in this box refers to the plant featured, and not necessarily to varieties or to similar species. When months or seasons are indicated, they can be taken as applying to temperate zones in the northern hemisphere.

Recommended temperatures are the minimum that the plants will tolerate at night in winter. Each box ends with a Warning alerting you to the plant's particular susceptibility to problems.

Beside each illustration you will find practical notes on avoiding or dealing with problems. These are an important feature of this section and will help you identify and treat the ailments, pests and diseases that are likely to afflict the featured plant.

Cross references at the bottom of each page guide you to further, detailed information, while unfamiliar terms are explained in the Glossary.

COMMON HYACINTH

Hyacinthus orientalis
Height: 15–23 cm
Spread: 7.5–13 cm

The stiff, upright, candle-like heads of the hyacinth grow 10–15 cm long and bear many waxy, six-petalled flowers that are highly scented. The true species is seldom grown; the many varieties are more popular and more profusely flowering. These come in many colours including white, yellow, pink, red, mauve and blue.

Indoor varieties for winter colour include 'City of Haarlem' (creamy yellow), 'Jan Bos' (cerise-pink), 'Delft Blue' (pale blue), 'Amethyst' (lilac-mauve), 'Bismark' (clear blue), and 'L'Innocence' (white).

Hyacinths normally flower outdoors during spring, but they can be forced into flower indoors during late winter. And bulbs that have been given an artificial cool period before being potted can be encouraged to flower at Christmas and into the New Year. These are known as specially-prepared bulbs.

Hyacinth bulbs are grown either singly in pots 7.5–10 cm wide, or in groups of about five bulbs in a bowl 15–20 cm wide and 10–13 cm deep. However, when several bulbs are grown in one bowl – and especially if they are different varieties – you cannot be certain they will flower together and grow to the same height.

To be sure of an impressive display, select several equal-sized plants whose flowers are starting to open. Either stand all the pots on a drainage layer of pebbles in one large container, with moist peat packed between them, or remove the pots and plant several in one bowl.

Do not economize by repotting forced bulbs the following autumn; they will not flower again indoors, though they might flower outdoors for several more years.

YELLOW
Variety illustrated:
'City of Haarlem'

CERISE-PINK
Variety illustrated:
'Jan Bos'

BLUE
Variety illustrated:
'Delft Blue'

SURVIVAL BASICS

Light and temperature: Bright light; 10°C (50°F) after shoots appear, slowly rising to 18°C (64°F) when flower buds show colour.

Watering and feeding: Keep compost moist, especially during flowering. Feeding is not necessary.

Compost and potting: In August or September, pot up bulbs in bulb fibre or John Innes potting compost No. 2, leaving the necks exposed. Water and keep in a cool (5°C/41°F), dark place until the leaf tips appear. Introduce gradually to the light.

Propagation: Fresh bulbs each year.

WARNING: Never buy bulbs that are soft, bruised or marked.

E. EUROPE
W. ASIA

After flowering indoors, allow the foliage to die down naturally in a frost-proof shed or greenhouse. In spring, plant the bulbs 15 cm deep around shrubs, where they will create spring and early summer colour. They can remain undisturbed for many years.

Flower buds wither or fail to open if compost is kept dry, watering is erratic or temperatures are excessively high.

Stunted growth is usually due to plants being brought into warmth and light before the roots are well developed and the shoots are well above the compost.

Foliage becomes yellow or limp if the plant is in a draught or watered erratically.

Hyacinthus orientalis 'Amethyst'

PESTS AND DISEASES
Stem and bulb
  eelworms
Narcissus fly maggots

• Bulbs pp.182–183

• Pests pp.194–196
• Checklists pp.212–217

SCREW PINE

Pandanus veitchii
Height: 60–75 cm
Spread: 60 cm

Glossy, bright green, spiny-edged leaves, striped and edged with cream, rise in a spiral from the screw pine's central stem. It is slow-growing and eventually becomes arched and palm-like.

This resilient and reliable houseplant is tough and tolerant of most conditions and will last for many years.

When mature, it is an impressive floorstanding plant. Position it away from children, as the spiny leaf edges are sharp. Also recommended:

P. baptistii, the blue screw pine: Grows 1.2–1.8 m high. The smooth-edged, bluish-green leaves have several bright yellow stripes down their centres.

SURVIVAL BASICS

Light and temperature: Bright, but indirect sunlight; winter temperatures of 13–21°C (55–70°F).

Watering and feeding: Keep compost barely moist in winter; water more in spring and summer. Add a weak liquid fertilizer every 3 weeks from spring to early autumn.

Compost and repotting: Use John Innes potting compost No. 2, or a peat-based mix. Repot in April, when potbound, usually every 2–3 years. Protect your hands with thick gloves.

Propagation: Remove and root basal shoots in spring.

WARNING: Do not let water accumulate in leaf joints.

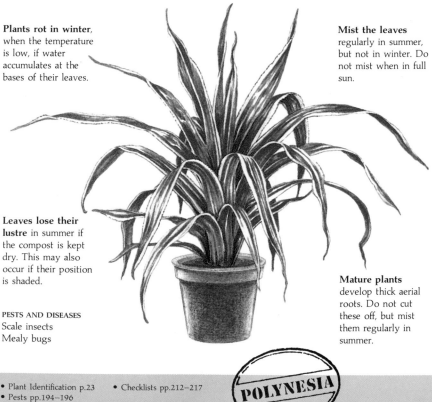

Plants rot in winter, when the temperature is low, if water accumulates at the bases of their leaves.

Mist the leaves regularly in summer, but not in winter. Do not mist when in full sun.

Leaves lose their lustre in summer if the compost is kept dry. This may also occur if their position is shaded.

PESTS AND DISEASES
Scale insects
Mealy bugs

Mature plants develop thick aerial roots. Do not cut these off, but mist them regularly in summer.

• Plant Identification p.23   • Checklists pp.212–217
• Pests pp.194–196

POLYNESIA

BOAT LILY

Rhoeo spathacea
Height: 30–38 cm
Spread: 30 cm

The long, sword-shaped leaves of this foliage plant are glossy and dark green on the upper surface and rich purple beneath. Together, they form a rosette.

The plant's common name comes from its small, white flowers cradled in purple, boat-shaped bracts about 5 cm long. The flowers may appear at any time and are short-lived, but the bracts last for many months.

If the boat lily is grown for show as a specimen plant, remove its sideshoots; otherwise, leave them alone.

Also recommended:
R. s. 'Vittata': Variegated, with thin, longitudinal cream stripes on the leaves.

SURVIVAL BASICS

Light and temperature: Lightly shaded, not direct sunlight; winter temperatures of 10–18°C (50–64°F).
Watering and feeding: In winter, keep compost just moist. Water freely in summer. Every 2 weeks, from April to September, add a weak liquid fertilizer.
Compost and repotting: Use John Innes potting compost No. 2, or a peat-based mix. Repot every spring.
Propagation: From late spring to midsummer, remove and pot up basal shoots.

WARNING: Keep warm and out of draughts.

Leaves scorch and turn brown if the plant is positioned in strong light, especially in winter.

Plants in 15 cm-wide pots do not need repotting. Topdress them by removing the top 18 mm of compost and replacing it with fresh.

Roots are soon damaged if the compost is kept too wet during summer or too dry in winter.

PESTS AND DISEASES
Greenfly
Mealy bugs

• Plant Identification p.27   • Propagation by Cuttings pp.176–178   • Pests pp.194–196   • Checklists pp.212–217

DAFFODIL

Narcissus spp.
Height: 38–50 cm
Spread: 7.5–13 cm

These harbingers of spring look delightful outdoors when grown in profusion. They can also be made to flower indoors in winter and early spring.

While many daffodil varieties can be grown in pots, the trumpet-flowered types, with their large bright flowers, are the most popular. Two excellent yellow-trumpet varieties are 'Dutch Master' and 'Golden Harvest'. For bicoloured flowers, choose 'Trousseau'; its blue-green foliage offsets the white and rosy-cream blooms. 'Queen of Bicolors' (pure white and chrome yellow) and 'Foresight' (white and lemon) are also recommended.

White-flowered types include 'Mount Hood' and 'Empress of Ireland'. For double-flowered varieties, try 'Texas' (cream-gold and tangerine) and 'Irene Copeland' (creamy-white).

If you prefer small flowers in bunched heads, then try the tazetta narcissus. Derived from *Narcissus tazetta*, it is closely associated with the poetaz narcissus which is a cross between *N. tazetta* and *N. poeticus*, the poet's narcissus. The two widely available tazetta varieties are 'Paper White' (white) and 'Soleil d'Or' (rich yellow petals, with an orange cup). Poetaz varieties include 'Cragford' (white and orange), 'Geranium' (white and rich orange) and 'Lauren's Koster' (white and lemon-yellow).

The cyclamineus narcissus grows 20–30 cm high, bearing tiny pendent flowers with long trumpets and petals that sweep backward. Recommended varieties include 'February Gold' (deep yellow), 'Peeping Tom' (bright yellow), and 'Tête-à-Tête' (yellow).

BICOLOURED
Petals and trumpet are of different colours.
Variety illustrated:
'Queen of Bicolors'

DOUBLE
Petals and trumpet are indistinguishable.
Variety illustrated:
'Irene Copeland'

POETAZ
Several small flowers on each stem.
Variety illustrated:
'Geranium'

SURVIVAL BASICS

Light and temperature: Bright light; winter temperatures of 7–10°C (45–50°F) after shoots appear, rising to 13°C (55°F) when flower buds are visible.

Watering and feeding: Keep moist. Feeding is not necessary.

Compost and potting: In late summer, pot up 5 or 7 bulbs in bulb fibre or John Innes potting compost in a bowl 15–20 cm wide and 7.5–10 cm deep. Leave tops exposed. Water and keep cool (5°C/40°F) and dark until leaf tips appear.

Propagation: Fresh bulbs each year.

WARNING: Do not leave bulbs in airtight bags; they will rot.

• Plant Identification p.10

Failure to flower, with buds turning brown, results from the growing medium having been too dry during the plant's 'cool period' when the roots were developing. Double varieties are especially susceptible to this.

Yellow leaves result from the bulbs being placed in a draught, or not receiving sufficient light.

Daffodils look best when several bulbs are planted in one container. They are not so effective grown singly in small pots.

EUROPE

Long, limp leaves develop because the bulbs were left for too long in the dark.

A layer of clean gravel on the surface of the compost not only enhances the display, it reduces evaporation from the surface.

Narcissus 'Dutch Master'

Stunted growth results from the bulbs having spent too short a period in a cool, dark place. Do not move the bulbs to a bright, warm position until the shoots are 2.5–5 cm high.

PESTS AND DISEASES
Stem and bulb
  eelworms
Narcissus fly maggots
Slugs

• Bulbs pp.182–183   • Pests pp.194–196
                       • Checklists pp.212–217

FLAMING SWORD

Vriesea splendens
Height: 38–45 cm
Spread: 23–30 cm

This boldly-striped bromeliad is strikingly decorative even when it is not in bloom. Flowering can be at any time from spring to early autumn, once the plant is several years old.

The evergreen, stiff, arching, dark green leaves, with dark purple cross-bands, are then dominated by a sword-like flower stem 60 cm high. The top half of this stem is formed of brilliant red bracts, or modified leaves, and bright yellow flowers 4–5 cm long, which last for several months.

Like those of many other bromeliads, the leaves form a rosette whose central urn must be kept full of water.

SURVIVAL BASICS

Light and temperature: Bright, but indirect sunlight; winter temperatures of 18–21°C (64–70°F).

Watering and feeding: In winter, keep compost barely moist, but otherwise water freely. Always keep the urn filled. From spring to early autumn, add weak liquid fertilizer every 3–4 weeks.

Compost and repotting: Use a lime-free peat-based mix, or equal parts peat and sharp sand. Repot in late spring, when the roots fill the pot.

Propagation: By offsets in late spring.

WARNING: Insecticides containing malathion can damage the plant.

Fine spider webs sometimes appear on the leaves if the atmosphere is dry. These are created by red spider mites, which suck the sap and cause fine speckling of the leaves. Do not use an insecticide to get rid of them. Instead, use a fine, dry brush to scrape them gently off the plant. If the infestation is severe, cut off the leaf close to the plant's centre.

Leaves become discoloured if the temperature is low and the atmosphere dry. Keep the temperature high, and mist the foliage daily, especially during summer.

Every 6–8 weeks, empty and refill the central urn with fresh water. In hardwater areas, use rainwater.

GUYANA

PESTS AND DISEASES
Mealy bugs
Red spider mites

4

ANGEL'S TEARS

Billbergia nutans
Height: 38–50 cm
Spread: 30–45 cm

The arching stems of this spectacular bromeliad bear long clusters of tubular green flowers, edged in blue, emerging from large pink bracts. The flowers appear throughout the summer amid erect, then drooping, narrow, dark green leaves with serrated edges. Like most bromeliads, its leaves form a rosette, though with angel's tears it is more grass-like.

Also recommended:

B. pyramidalis, the summer torch: Apple-green or grey leaves and red flowers tipped with blue.

B. zebrina: Wide, purplish-bronze or dark green leaves are cross-banded in silvery-grey. Pendulous, deep purple flowers.

SURVIVAL BASICS

Light and temperature: Bright, indirect sunlight; winter temperatures of 13–23 °C (55–73 °F).

Watering and feeding: In winter, keep compost nearly dry, but in summer water freely. Avoid waterlogging; allow the surface to dry out between waterings. From late spring to autumn, add weak liquid fertilizer every 2–3 weeks.

Compost and repotting: Use lime-free John Innes potting compost No. 2 or 3. Repot in the spring, when potbound.

Propagation: By offsets in spring.

WARNING: Low temperatures and wet compost in winter rot the roots.

If recommended temperatures cannot be achieved, keep the potting mix slightly drier. But low temperatures over a long period will damage the plant.

Scorched and dead leaves occur when the plant is placed in strong light. Move it to light shade and cut off damaged leaves.

S. AMERICA

Every 6–8 weeks tip out the water from the urn, replenishing it with fresh. In hardwater areas, use rainwater.

PESTS AND DISEASES
Red spider mites
Mealy bugs
Scale insects

• Plant Identification p.11   • Propagation by Offsets p.179   • Bromeliads pp.190–191   • Pests pp.194–196   • Checklists pp.212–217

AMARYLLIS

Hippeastrum hybrida
Height: 30–45 cm
Spread: 15–23 cm

HIPPEASTRUM HYBRIDA
A Christmas-flowering hybrid.
Variety illustrated:
'Apple Blossom'

A plant ideal for a sunny windowsill. The giant, trumpet-shaped flowers produced on tall stems appear mainly in spring, although specially prepared bulbs will flower at Christmas.

Christmas-flowering varieties include 'Apple Blossom' (pale pink, lighter in the throat), 'Minerva' (white, edged and veined in brick-red) and 'Mont Blanc' (pure white, tinged green in the throat). Those for late winter and spring flowering include 'Fiery Diamond' (intense orange-red), 'Excelsior' (clear orange) and 'Queen of Sheba' (glowing deep rose with a hint of lilac). Unprepared Christmas-flowering types will also flower in early spring.

When the active growth period has ended, stop watering and allow the foliage to die down. Prepare the plant for its dormant period by removing the dried foliage, then store the bulb in a dark, dry place at about 10°C (50°F) until you start it back into growth.

To encourage new growth, first wash away the top 2–3 cm of potting mix. Top up with fresh mix enriched with a teaspoon of bonemeal. This will provide the bulb with nourishment without disturbing its roots. Remember that the top half of the bulb should protrude above the surface. Do not be disappointed if the bulb is slow to show signs of life. It may be several weeks before new growth (probably the flower bud) emerges.

The common name amaryllis often leads to confusion between *Hippeastrum* and the outdoor plant *Amaryllis belladonna*, the belladonna lily. This can be grown outdoors only in a warm, sheltered spot or in a conservatory.

SURVIVAL BASICS

Light and temperature: Bright, direct or indirect light; 18°C (64°F) after the shoots appear.

Watering and feeding: During active growth, soak the compost with tepid water. Let the surface dry out between waterings. Feed every 2 weeks with a weak liquid fertilizer.

Compost and repotting: Pot up the Christmas-flowering bulbs in November; late winter and spring types in September/October. Use John Innes potting compost No. 1.

Propagation: By offsets when repotting.

WARNING: Leave the plant in good light until the leaves die down.

• Plant Identification p.10

Failure to flower, or the development of poor blooms, results from inadequate feeding the previous year, and removing plants from a sunny position after they have flowered.

With care, amaryllis bulbs will last for many years.

Bulbs are killed by cold water, so use tepid water, especially for winter-flowering types.

HYBRID

Hippeastrum 'Safari'

PESTS AND DISEASES
Mealy bugs
Red spider mites

• Propagation by Offsets
  p.179
• Bulbs pp.182–183
• Pests pp.194–196
• Checklists pp.212–217

PARTRIDGE-BREASTED ALOE

Aloe variegata
Height: 10–15 cm
Spread: 10–13 cm

The stiff, triangular-shaped, tooth-edged leaves of this succulent overlap. They are dark grey-green, 13 cm long and irregularly marked in white. In March or April, a 30 cm-upright shoot is produced, bearing pink or scarlet, tubular, bell-shaped flowers arranged in a loose head.

Never plant an aloe in a bottle garden. The high humidity and constantly wet compost will quickly make it rot and die. Also recommended:

A. v. 'Sabra': Miniature with dainty pink flowers borne in late summer.

A. aristata, the lace aloe: Dark green leaves are peppered with grey-white, wart-like swellings.

SURVIVAL BASICS

Light and temperature: Bright, indirect sunlight; winter temperatures of 5–7°C (41–45°F).

Watering and feeding: Keep compost dry in winter. In summer, water frequently, but let compost dry out between waterings. From April to September, feed monthly with a weak liquid fertilizer.

Compost and repotting: Repot in spring in a gritty, loam-based mix. Do not change the depth of planting. Add grit to the surface to prevent water collecting around the plant.

Propagation: By offsets in spring.

WARNING: Keep out of draughts, especially in winter.

Leaves will rot if water accumulates in leaf bases.

Roots will rot in winter if the plant is in too cool a room and the compost is continually saturated. If necessary, dry the roots by removing the pot and wrapping the rootball in several sheets of newspaper for a few days.

PESTS AND DISEASES
Red spider mites
Mealy bugs
Root mealy bugs

• Plant Identification p.25   • Propagation by Offsets p.179   • Succulents pp.184–185   • Pests pp.194–196   • Checklists pp.212–217

EARTH STAR

Cryptanthus bivittatus
Height: 7.5 cm
Spread: 13–20 cm

This tiny bromeliad's star-shaped rosettes of lance-shaped, toothed and wavy leaves rise direct from the surface of the compost. They are pale green, striped in dark green.

The earth star does not form an urn at its centre because, in the wild, it grows on moss-covered logs on tropical forest floors. An alternative to planting it in a pot is to wrap the rootball in sphagnum moss and tie it to a log or piece of gnarled bark. Mist the moss regularly to keep the roots moist.

Also recommended:
C. acaulis, the starfish plant: Wavy, spiny-edged, pale green leaves form flat stars.

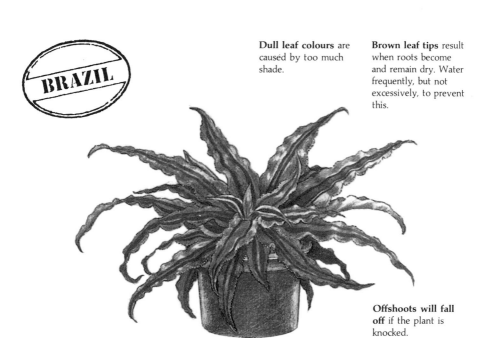

BRAZIL

Dull leaf colours are caused by too much shade.

Brown leaf tips result when roots become and remain dry. Water frequently, but not excessively, to prevent this.

Offshoots will fall off if the plant is knocked.

• Plant Identification p.24   • Propagation by Offsets
p.179   • Bromeliads pp.190–191
• Checklists pp.212–217

URN PLANT

Aechmea fasciata
Height: 45–60 cm
Spread: 30–45 cm

The urn plant is the easiest of all bromeliads to grow as a houseplant. The large, stiff, strap-like leaves arch outward to reveal attractive silvery white mottling or cross-banding. The leaves form a large urn that acts as a reservoir and helps to satisfy the plant's moisture needs.

During August, in mature plants, a flower stem rises from the centre of the urn; this bears a 10–15 cm-long, cone-shaped flower head, formed of tubular blue flowers, later turning rose, amid sharply pointed pink bracts. The flowers soon fade, but the bracts last for about four months.

Young plants can be grown on small, bare branches secured in a sturdy base – these are called 'bromeliad trees'. Remove the plants from their pots, wrap the roots in sphagnum moss and secure them with plastic-covered wire to the upper surface of the branches.

The coral berry, *A. fulgens discolor*, grows to about 38 cm high and 30 cm wide. Its soft, leathery, strap-like leaves are olive green above, reddish-purple beneath, and are covered with white powdery scales. During August and September, it develops an oval, 10–15 cm-long, head of waxen-blue flowers, followed by long-lasting, reddish berries.

The Amazonian zebra plant, *A. chantinii*, grows as high as 75–90 cm and as wide as 75 cm. As with *A. fasciata*, the dark green leaves are banded with silver scales. In autumn, it bears long, oval heads formed of yellow and bright scarlet flowers. Not so hardy as other aechmeas, it needs a higher temperature, about 18°C (64°F), and greater humidity.

AECHMEA FULGENS DISCOLOR
Blue flowers, long-lasting red berries and purple-backed leaves.

AECHMEA CHANTINII
Yellow and scarlet flowers, long-lasting red bracts and broad-banded leaves.

SURVIVAL BASICS

Light and temperature: Bright, indirect sunlight; winter temperatures of 13–18°C (55–64°F).

Watering and feeding: Keep compost moist, but not waterlogged, in winter. Water freely in summer, and keep the urn filled. From late spring to early autumn, add a weak liquid fertilizer every 2 weeks.

Compost and repotting: Use a lime-free, peat-based mix. In late spring, repot potbound plants.

Propagation: Remove and pot-up offsets when 7.5–10 cm high.

WARNING: Dry foliage loses its colour, so mist the plant daily.

In dry conditions, stand the plant on a layer of pebbles in a shallow tray filled with pebbles and water to create extra humidity.

Pale brown patches on leaves are caused by strong sunlight in summer. Move the plant to a slightly shaded position.

Leaves can absorb extra food if you add a weak liquid fertilizer to the water used for misting every 10–14 days.

Empty and refill the urn every 6–8 weeks, using rainwater in hardwater areas.

Aechmea fasciata

• Propagation by Offsets p.179

• Bromeliads pp.190–191
• Checklists p.212–217

SCARLET STAR

Guzmania lingulata
Height: 30 cm
Spread: 38–50 cm

This distinctive bromeliad has shiny, tapering, strap-like, metallic-green leaves arranged in a rosette. The flower heads appear thoughout summer and grow to about 30 cm. They are cylindrical and are formed of small yellow flowers almost surrounded by red bracts.
Also recommended:
G. monostachya, the striped torch: Glossy, smooth-edged, strap-like, green leaves. Produces torch-like heads of white flowers and greenish-white bracts with brownish-purple stripes.
G. sanguinea: Each central leaf is tinged red at the tip and to half its length, the rest being yellow or light green.

SURVIVAL BASICS

Light and temperature: Light shade; 16–24°C (61–75°F) − the higher temperature is needed to bring the plant into flower.
Watering and feeding: Keep compost just moist in winter; water freely in summer. Use rainwater. Keep the urn filled, emptying and replenishing it every 6–8 weeks. Add a weak liquid fertilizer to the water every 4 weeks in summer.
Compost and repotting: Use a peat-based mix, plus coarse sand.
Propagation: Remove and pot up offsets in spring.

WARNING: Overwatering in winter causes the plant to rot.

W. INDIES
–BRAZIL

Guzmanias flower only once, but they produce offsets that can be removed and repotted each spring.

Greenfly attack soft leaf tips and flowers. Spray with a pyrethrum-based insecticide; or use an insecticide based on malathion watered on to the compost.

Brown leaves result from roots rotting in waterlogged compost, especially in winter. Remove the rootball from the pot and wrap it in several sheets of newspaper to dry it out.

PESTS AND DISEASES
Greenfly

• Plant Identification p.23   • Propagation by Offsets p.179   • Bromeliads pp.190–191   • Checklists pp.212–217
• Pests pp.194–196

S.E. USA

Always position floor-standing spineless yuccas where they cannot be damaged by children or pets.

Wilting plants could be caused by a potting mix saturated with water, especially in winter. Remove the rootball from the pot to allow the compost to dry out. Too dry a mix could have the same effect.

Misting the leaves is unnecessary. Indeed, in winter and at low temperatures, it can be detrimental.

PESTS AND DISEASES
Mealy bugs
Scale insects
Botrytis

SPINELESS YUCCA

Yucca elephantipes
Height: 0.9–1.8 m
Spread: 30–60 cm

Few foliage plants are as eye-catching as the yucca. The stiff green leaves sprout in a rosette from the top of its upright, woody stem. Eventually, the leaves arch, then fall off, increasing the length of stem. Outdoors, mature plants produce spikes of ivory-white flowers in late summer. Flowering is rare in indoor specimens.

The Spanish bayonet or dagger plant, *Y. aloifolia*, has a forbidding appearance, with its sharply-pointed, deep green leaves serrated at the edges. It is best reserved for homes without young children or pets. The trunk grows 0.9–1.2 m high, with leaves arranged in a rosette at its top. Yellow-white flowers, usually tinged purple and borne in long spikes, appear from mid- to late summer.

SURVIVAL BASICS

Light and temperature: Full sun; minimum temperature of 7°C (45°F).
Watering and feeding: Keep compost barely moist in winter. In summer, water freely. From April to September, add a weak liquid fertilizer every 3–4 weeks.
Compost and repotting: Use John Innes potting compost No. 2. Repot in spring when potbound.
Propagation: Pot up offshoots in spring. Alternatively, cut up the stems of old plants into 10–13 cm-sections. Pot them up and keep at 24–27°C (75–81°F).

WARNING: Insufficient light will cause discoloration of the leaves.

• Plant Identification p.25   • Propagation by   • Propagation by Offsets   • Diseases p.197
• Pests pp.194–196   Cuttings p.181   p.179   • Checklists pp.212–217

BLUSHING BROMELIAD

Neoregelia carolinae
Height: 30 cm
Spread: 30–38 cm

This striking, symmetrical, long-lived bromeliad is usually found, in the wild, growing on the rain forest floor or on the lower branches of a tree which it uses as an anchor rather than a food source.

Glossy, green, saw-edged, strap-like leaves radiate from its centre to form a water-holding urn. This is a feature of most bromeliads, which obtain nourishment from the water and airborne debris that collect in it.

When the plant is about to flower, which can be at any time, the central part of the rosette of leaves becomes purple or bright red, as if it were blushing. The rosette flattens and a tightly-packed flower head rises up through a gap 5 cm wide. Soon after, violet-blue flowers, 2.5 cm wide, appear.

One of the most popular varieties is *N. c.* 'Tricolor' which has bright green leaves with cream and rose-pink stripes. At flowering time, the entire plant becomes pinky-red and often remains so for several months.

Another attractive variety is *N. c.* 'Marechallii' which has broad, strap-like, spiny-edged, bright green leaves. At flowering time, the lower half of each leaf turns bright red.

The fingernail plant, *N. spectabilis*, also develops a central urn, with leathery, metallic-green leaves up to 30 cm long which form a rosette 60 cm across. The leaves are tipped with bright red spots, 2.5 cm long, that give rise to the common name. At flowering time, the rosette becomes rose-red, with small blue flowers encircled by purple-brown modified leaves known as bracts.

NEOREGELIA SPECTABILIS:
Leaf tips have a red spot reminiscent of a painted fingernail.

NEOREGELIA CAROLINAE 'MARECHALLII'
The lower half of the leaves blush red before the plant's violet flowers appear.

SURVIVAL BASICS

Light and temperature: Bright light, with some direct sunlight; 10–21°C (50–70°F). A high temperature encourages flowering.

Watering and feeding: Water when compost dries out. Avoid continual saturation. Keep the urn full. Add a weak liquid fertilizer every 2–3 weeks. Mist the foliage daily.

Compost and repotting: Use 2 parts peat-based mix to 1 part coarse sand. Repot in May, when potbound, every 3 or 4 years.

Propagation: In May or June, pot up offshoots that are 10 cm high.

WARNING: Dry compost makes leaves shrivel and curl.

• Plant Identification p.22

At flowering time the rosette flattens and the flower head emerges from the central urn.

BRAZIL

Leaves lose their lustre in winter if the plant is kept too cold or in a draught.

Leaves become scorched at their tips if left in strong sunlight during summer.

Thoroughly soak the compost at each watering.

Neoregelia carolinae 'Tricolor'

PESTS AND DISEASES
Mealy bugs
Scale insects

• Propagation by Offsets p.179

• Bromeliads p.190–191

• Pests pp.194–196

• Checklists pp.212–217

PINEAPPLE PLANT

Ananas comosus
Height: 60–90 cm
Spread: 40–45 cm

Pineapple plants are the only bromeliads to have been commercially exploited on a large scale. They look superb, but do not expect them to produce edible fruits indoors. Mature plants might bear fruits, but they are usually inedible and best considered as ornamental features.

In summer, the long, spiny-edged, grey-green leaves arch to reveal a short stem, bearing a 7.5 cm-wide, purple flower head below a tuft of smaller leaves. Also recommended:
A. c. variegatus: Green, sharp-edged leaves have light yellow edges and pink tips.
A. sagenaria striatus: Green leaves have creamy stripes along red, spiny edges.

SURVIVAL BASICS

Light and temperature: Full sunlight; winter temperatures of 15–23 °C (59–73 °F).
Watering and feeding: Keep compost moist in winter, but not continually saturated. Water freely in summer, allowing the surface to dry out between waterings. From April to October, add a weak liquid fertilizer every 3–4 weeks.
Compost and repotting: Use John Innes potting compost No. 2, with extra peat. Repot in late spring.
Propagation: In spring, remove and pot up offshoots.

WARNING: Mature plants that fruit may topple unless supported.

Plants that do bear fruit have a short life. After fruiting, the stout stem dies back and the rosette withers. Sucker-like shoots from the plant's base will develop into new plants. Remove them and pot them up.

An easy way to propagate a pineapple plant is to cut off the top third of a mature pineapple and suspend the cut base in shallow water. In a few weeks, when roots have formed, it can be potted up.

Several large pebbles in the base will stabilize top-heavy pots holding mature fruiting plants.

BRAZIL COLOMBIA

• Plant Identification p.23   • Propagation by Offsets p.179   • Checklists pp.212–217

MOTHER-IN-LAW'S TONGUE

Sansevieria trifasciata
Height: 38–45 cm
Spread: 15–20 cm

The stiff, upright, sword-shaped and sharply-tipped leaves are dark green, with mottled, greyish-white cross-bands. Mother-in-law's tongue is an attractive and impressive-looking plant. This, plus the fact that it is one of the toughest houseplants, accounts for its popularity.

S. t. 'Laurentii', with leaves distinctively edged in creamy-yellow, is the most common form. Both of these plants, when grown in large pots, may eventually reach 1 m high, but this is unusual.
Also recommended:
S. t. 'Hahnii', the bird's nest sansevieria: Forms a 15 cm-high nest of triangular, spirally arranged, deep green leaves with lighter cross-bands.

Variegated plants revert to all-green if left in a shady position. Move to a bright windowsill.

Yellowing leaves that eventually die are caused by keeping the potting mix too wet, especially during winter. Allow it to dry out and move the plant to a warmer spot.

PESTS AND DISEASES
Mealy bugs
Scale insects

SURVIVAL BASICS

Light and temperature: Bright sun; winter temperatures of 10–16°C (50–61°F).
Watering and feeding: Keep compost barely moist in winter. From spring to autumn, allow the compost to dry out between waterings.
Compost and repotting: Use John Innes potting compost No. 2 or a peat-based type. Repot in spring.
Propagation: In summer, by offshoots; or by division when repotting. Plants without coloured edges can be increased from leaf cuttings.

WARNING: Low temperatures, below 7°C (45°F), and waterlogged compost are fatal.

• Propagation by Cuttings pp.176–178

• Propagation by Division p.179

• Propagation by Offsets p.179

• Pests pp.194–196
• Checklists pp.212–217

CROTON

Codiaeum variegatum pictum
Height: 45–60 cm
Spread: 25–38 cm

Few foliage plants are more colourful than the crotons. This is reflected in one of their common names, Joseph's coat, which was, of course, 'of many colours'.

The green leathery leaves of crotons vary widely in colour, shape and size. They may be veined in yellow or pink, or spotted and blotched in colours from yellow to nearly black. These colours may remain the same or darken with age. The leaves can be long or short, broad or narrow, straight or wavy-edged, shallowly or deeply lobed. The range of crotons is enormous, and several new varieties become available each year.

Selected and named forms include 'Reidii', with dark green leaves shaded yellow to pinkish-red, and highlighted with dark yellow veins. 'Black Prince' has broad, oval, blackish-green leaves, flecked with orange, scarlet and yellow.

'Disraeli' has three-lobed, medium green leaves mottled with yellow. The undersides are flushed dark red.

'Carrierei' has yellow leaves when young; these turn dark green with red centres. 'Norma' has deep green leaves with red veins. Some have deep yellow blotches on a vivid green background.

'Bravo' has long, spoon-shaped leaves with deeply indented, rounded edges. Most leaves have yellow blotches on a green background, but those at the base of the plant also have red edges.

'Craigii' is grown for its deeply-lobed leaves which are beautifully coloured with bright, rich, golden-yellow veins on a deep green background. At the ends of the leaves, a wide central lobe is flanked by two narrow lobes.

CODIAEUM VARIEGATUM 'CARRIEREI'
Young, yellow-green leaves become dark green with red centres when mature.

CODIAEUM VARIEGATUM 'DISRAELI'
Three-lobed leaves have yellow blotches and reddish undersides.

CODIAEUM VARIEGATUM 'GOLD FINGER'
Green, lance-shaped leaves have a bold yellow stripe along the midrib.

SURVIVAL BASICS

Light and temperature: Bright, indirect sunlight; winter temperature of 15°C (59°F).

Watering and feeding: Water sparingly in winter, freely in summer; never let compost remain saturated. From April to September, add a weak liquid fertilizer every 2 weeks.

Compost and repotting: Use John Innes potting compost No. 2. Repot in spring, when potbound.

Propagation: In spring, take 7.5–10 cm-long tip cuttings from the side shoots.

WARNING: Both low and rapidly changing temperatures cause the leaves to fall.

• Plant Identification pp.21, 25

Leaves brown at their tips if the potting mix is too dry. If the edges brown, check that the temperature is not too low.

Leaves become scorched if the plant is placed in strong sunlight, especially in summer.

MALAYSIA

Faded colour occurs because the light is poor, especially in winter. Move to a brighter position.

Codiaeum variegatum 'Reidii'

PESTS AND DISEASES
Mealy bugs
Scale insects
Red spider mites

• Propagation by
  Cuttings pp.176–178

• Pests pp.194–196
• Checklists pp.212–217

UMBRELLA PLANT

Cyperus alternifolius
Height: 45–60 cm
Spread: 25–38 cm

This water-loving plant bears long, thin, upright, dark green stems with umbrella-shaped tufts of narrow, leaf-like bracts at the top. The real leaves form a clump around the base.

From July to September, a cluster of grass-like flower heads appears above the bracts. Flowers are yellow at first but turn dull brown as the seeds mature.

Also recommended:

C. a. 'Variegatus': Stems and leaves have creamy-white stripes.

C. a. 'Gracilis': Miniature; good for confined places as it grows 38–45 cm high.

C. diffusus: Smaller than *C. alternifolius*, with denser umbrella heads.

SURVIVAL BASICS

Light and temperature: Bright, indirect sunlight; winter temperatures of 10–15°C (50–59°F).

Watering and feeding: Keep compost constantly moist by standing the pot in a water-filled container. From April to September, add a weak liquid fertilizer every 2 weeks.

Compost and repotting: Use John Innes potting compost No. 2, plus a few pieces of charcoal to keep it fresh. Repot every spring.

Propagation: When repotting, divide congested plants. This is a messy job best tackled outdoors.

WARNING: Winter temperatures below 10°C (50°F) are fatal.

A wise precaution in winter is to keep plants at the upper end of the recommended temperature range.

Brown tips to the leaves indicate a lack of moisture at the roots or a dry atmosphere. Give more water and mist the foliage frequently.

Yellowing and wilting leaves also indicate a lack of water. Cut out these stems and give the plant more water.

PESTS AND DISEASES
Greenfly

• Plant Identification p.29   • Propagation by Division p.179   • Pests pp.194–196   • Checklists pp.212–217

FALSE ARALIA

Dizygotheca elegantissima
Height: 0.75–1.2 m
Spread: 38–50 cm

This graceful and distinctive plant is most attractive when young. Its delicate, finger-like leaves are formed of seven to ten, leathery, narrow, saw-edged, coppery-red leaflets.

With age, the leaves slowly change to very dark green, widening and becoming coarse, so the plant loses its graceful appearance. By that time, however, it has usually shed many of its lower leaves and is best replaced.

Plants that have lost their lower leaves, and are not too woody and old, can be given a new lease of life in spring by cutting back the stems to compost level. Fresh stems then develop from the base.

SURVIVAL BASICS

Light and temperature: Bright, indirect light; winter temperatures of 18–23 °C (64–73 °F).
Watering and feeding: Keep compost barely moist in winter; water more in summer but do not saturate. From April to September, add a weak liquid fertilizer every 2 weeks.
Compost and repotting: Use John Innes potting compost No. 2 or a peat-based mix. Repot in spring, when potbound.
Propagation: Take stem-tip cuttings 10 cm long in spring.

WARNING: Low temperatures and wet compost spell disaster. Avoid sudden changes in temperature.

Drooping leaves are caused by either too much or too little water. Check the potting mix and remedy accordingly.

NEW HEBRIDES

Small, brown, blister-like spots on the undersides of the leaves are caused by scale insects. Scrape them off and spray with a systemic insecticide.

PESTS AND DISEASES
Scale insects

• Plant Identification p.29   • Propagation by Cuttings pp.176–178   • Pests pp.194–196   • Checklists pp.212–217

CHRYSANTHEMUM

Chrysanthemum spp.
Height: 20–38 cm
Spread: 20–30 cm

SINGLE
Chrysanthemum
hybrid

MARGUERITE
Chrysanthemum
frutescens hybrid

POMPON
Chrysanthemum
hybrid

Throughout the year these familiar plants are sold in their millions. As houseplants they are usually bought just as the flowers are bursting from their buds and revealing colour.

When grown outdoors, they usually start to flower in late summer or autumn, when the days are getting shorter; indeed, they are called short-day plants. However, by manipulating the hours of light and dark, and by providing the right temperatures, professional growers can encourage chrysanthemums to flower throughout the year. Plants produced in this way are known as all-year-round chrysanthemums.

All-year-round plants are either grown in large beds in greenhouses, to produce blooms suitable for sale as cut flowers, or in pots that can be sold when the buds show colour.

Many pot-grown all-year-round chrysanthemums have also been treated with hormones to restrict their growth, making them more suitable for growing in small pots. Once they have flowered, the plants are best discarded. Even if they are planted outdoors, they will probably flower only in the following autumn, and may then grow much taller.

These plants are varieties, derived mainly from *Chrysanthemum morifolium* and *C. indicum*, and are available in colours including yellow, orange, red, pink and white. Each pot has several plants in it, so that a bushy, branching, marketable plant can be produced quickly and the pot filled with leaves and flowers. The plants will usually remain in flower for six to eight weeks.

SURVIVAL BASICS

Light and temperature: Bright, indirect sunlight; a windowsill in winter offers a good position, but avoid bright sunlight in summer; 10–15°C (50–59°F). Avoid higher temperatures in order to prolong the flowering period.

Watering and feeding: Keep compost constantly moist. No feeding is necessary.

Compost and repotting: Neither of these is necessary if plants are discarded after flowering.

Propagation: Raising pot-grown plants is best left to professionals.

WARNING: High temperatures and dry compost damage plants.

• Plant Identification p.9

The flowering period will be shortened if the temperature is kept too high, since the process of bud opening will be speeded up.

Flower buds will not open if the plant was raised incorrectly and marketed before the buds were formed. Buy only those plants with buds showing colour. Green buds often fail to open.

Hot, dry weather will encourage an attack of red spider mites. Keep the plant in moderate temperatures and mist the leaves regularly to deter the pests.

Wilting leaves are usually a sign that the plant has been underwatered.

Chrysanthemum morifolium

PESTS AND DISEASES
Greenfly
Red spider mites
Thrips

• Pests pp.194–196
• Checklists pp.212–217

SPIDER PLANT

Chlorophytum comosum
Height: 15—25 cm
Spread: 25—45 cm

This quick-growing plant produces a wealth of narrow, arching, medium green leaves. It is usually seen in a variegated form, such as 'Variegatum', which has green leaves edged in white, or 'Vittatum', which has green leaves with a central white stripe.

In summer, long, thin, stiffly arching, white stems appear, bearing small, white, starry flowers followed by small plantlets. These stems can reach up to 75 cm long.
Also recommended:
C. capense: Long, narrow, pale to medium green leaves, often with wide, white, central stripes.

SURVIVAL BASICS

Light and temperature: Indirect sunlight; winter temperatures of 7—10°C (45—50°F).
Watering and feeding: In winter, keep compost barely moist. In summer, water freely. From April to October, add a liquid fertilizer every week.
Compost and repotting: Use John Innes potting compost No. 2, or a peat-based mix. Repot in spring.
Propagation: Divide congested plants when repotting or peg plantlets into small pots of compost.

WARNING: Repot the plant before the tuberous roots force the rootball out of the pot.

Brown leaf tips result from lack of food or dry air. Brown streaks on the leaves in winter are caused by low temperatures and too much water.

Pale, limp leaves in winter are caused by too little light and too high a temperature.

PESTS AND DISEASES
Red spider mites
Mealy bugs

KANGAROO VINE

Cissus antarctica
Height: 1.6–2.4 m
Spread: 60–90 cm

AUSTRALIA

This evergreen climber will grow into a large plant, 4.5–5.4 m high, when in a greenhouse border, but in a pot 15–20 cm wide it is more manageable. The glossy, dark green, heart-shaped leaves are scalloped and spiny-edged. They grow about 10 cm long and 5 cm wide.
Also recommended:
C. discolor, the begonia vine: Elongated, heart-shaped leaves are vivid green and marbled silvery-white with purple. The undersides are maroon-red.
C. rhombifolia, the grape ivy: Dark green leaves, arranged in threes, are diamond-shaped with scalloped, spiny edges.

Leaf tips shrivel and turn brown if the air is dry. Gently mist the leaves, but not in strong sunlight.

Blistered, brown, falling leaves are caused by strong, direct sunlight.

Drooping and wilting leaves in winter indicate too low a temperature. Leaves also wilt if the compost is too wet or too dry.

Large plants with plenty of foliage need a good circulation of air around them to prevent mildew.

SURVIVAL BASICS

Light and temperature: Bright, but indirect sunlight; winter temperatures of 7–10°C (45–50°F).
Watering and feeding: In winter, keep compost just moist, but water freely in summer. Do not keep compost continually saturated. From April to September, add a weak liquid fertilizer every 2–3 weeks.
Compost and repotting: Use John Innes potting compost No. 2. Repot in spring, when potbound.
Propagation: In late spring and midsummer, take stem cuttings 7.5–10 cm long.

WARNING: Direct sunlight will damage leaves.

PESTS AND DISEASES
Mildew
Greenfly
Red spider mites
Mealy bugs

• Plant Identification p.18   • Propagation by Cuttings pp.176–178   • Pests pp.194–196   • Diseases p.197   • Checklists pp.212–217

POINSETTIA

Euphorbia pulcherrima
Height: 40–45 cm
Spread: 30–38 cm

This widely-grown Christmas gift plant is a deciduous shrub prized for its brightly coloured, leaf-like bracts. These are usually bright red, but creamy white and pink varieties are also available.

In their native habitat, poinsettias are normally 1.2–1.5 m high, but growers in Scandinavia and California have produced smaller strains for indoor use.

Summer treatment: Plants can be saved from year to year, but they will get increasingly larger. After the bracts have faded and the real leaves fallen, cut back the stems to 10 cm high. Place the plant in a frostproof, shady position, keeping the compost almost dry.

In late spring, repot the plant into the same – or fractionally larger – size pot. Remove some of the old potting mix and replace with fresh. Then drench the compost with water and place in bright, indirect light at 13–15°C (55–59°F). Keep the compost moist and fresh shoots will develop. When these are 7.5–10 cm high, remove all but four or five of the strongest ones and use them as cuttings.

To make sure these short-day plants flower at Christmas, you must control the period of light to which they are exposed. Place a large, black polythene bag over the plant from early evening to late morning, so that it receives 14 hours of darkness for eight weeks. This makes the flower buds develop. Then place the plant in indirect sunlight at 15°C (59°F).

The crown of thorns, *E. milii*, has stiff, woody, spreading, thorny stems and small, medium green leaves. In winter, it bears small, yellow flowers surrounded by two petal-like, red or yellow bracts.

EUPHORBIA MILII 'TANANARIVAE'
Bright yellow bracts with tiny yellow flowers. Reaches 38–45 cm high and 30–38 cm wide.

SURVIVAL BASICS

Light and temperature: Bright light in winter, diffused sunlight in summer; 13–16°C (55–61°F) in winter when flowering.

Watering and feeding: Keep compost moist when in flower. See also *Summer treatment*, left. From May to September, add a weak liquid fertilizer every 2 weeks.

Compost and repotting: Use John Innes potting compost No. 2. Repotting – see *Summer treatment*.

Propagation: Take 7.5–10 cm-long stem-tip cuttings.

WARNING: Cold draughts or rapid changes in temperature cause leaves to fall.

Wilting leaves are usually due to a waterlogged soil. Allow the surface to dry out before watering further. If the whole rootball is saturated, remove the pot to allow rapid drying. Dry compost also causes wilting.

Leaf edges turn yellow, then brown, if the air is too dry. The leaf-like bracts may also fall off. Keep the air humid and mist the plant daily. This also helps to deter red spider mites.

Leaves may fall if the plant is kept in poor light.

Euphorbia pulcherrima

PESTS AND DISEASES
Red spider mites
Greenfly
Mealy bugs
Botrytis

• Propagation by Cuttings pp.176–178

• Pests pp.194–196
• Diseases p.197

• Checklists pp.212–217

ASPARAGUS FERN

Asparagus densiflorus 'Sprengeri'
Height: 30 cm
Spread: 75–90 cm

This arching, evergreen plant looks good in an indoor hanging basket or when cascading over the edge of a high shelf. It has graceful, feathery, needle-like, glossy green foliage on long, thin, wiry stems.

The plume asparagus, *A. d.* 'Meyeri', has upright, arching stems, up to 60 cm long, densely covered with bright green, needle-like leaves.

Another asparagus fern, *A. setaceus*, also widely known as *A. plumosus*, is frequently used by florists as background foliage for floral bouquets or button holes. The stiff, upright stems have medium green, lace-like leaves that grow in horizontal tiers.

SURVIVAL BASICS

Light and temperature: Semi-shade, avoid direct sunlight; winter temperatures of 10–13 °C (50–55 °F).
Watering and feeding: Keep compost just moist in winter, watering freely in summer. If the temperature falls to 7 °C (45 °F) in winter, give even less water. From April to September, add a weak liquid fertilizer every 2 weeks.
Compost and repotting: Use John Innes potting compost No. 2. Repot in spring, when potbound.
Propagation: Divide congested plants in spring or early summer.

WARNING: Poor light causes yellowing foliage and falling leaves.

If leaves turn brown at their edges, check that the compost is not too dry; otherwise, the leaves will turn yellow and fall.

Yellowing foliage on young shoots indicates that the plant is in poor light and too high a temperature. Position the plant in better light, reduce the temperature and feed regularly.

Old shoots with yellow leaves are best cut out at their bases. This encourages the development of young shoots. Cut the shoots back in spring and feed them regularly.

PESTS AND DISEASES
Red spider mites
Scale insects

• Plant Identification p.17   • Propagation by Division p.179   • Ferns pp.186–187   • Pests pp.194–196   • Checklists pp.212–217

BUTTON FERN

Pellaea rotundifolia
Height: 25—30 cm
Spread: 30—38 cm

This low-growing fern bears arching, wiry stems 20—25 cm long, with small, slightly waxy, dark green, leathery, button-like leaves. Each leaf is about 1.5 cm across and has serrated edges. The plant is unusual, resilient and quite unlike normal ferns in appearance.

A flourishing specimen has an attractive shape and the colour is enhanced by a white container. Make sure you position it where it can be easily watered.

If you grow the button fern in an indoor hanging basket, line the basket thickly with sphagnum moss. It needs a drip-tray to catch excess water.

SURVIVAL BASICS

Light and temperature: Indirect sunlight; winter temperatures of 15—18°C (59—64°F). Avoid temperatures over 23°C (73°F).
Watering and feeding: In winter, keep compost just moist. Water freely in summer, but avoid saturation. From May to September, add a weak liquid fertilizer every 2 weeks.
Compost and repotting: Use a peat-based mix. Repot in spring, when potbound.
Propagation: Divide congested plants in spring.

WARNING: Low temperatures, dry compost and insufficient humidity are fatal.

Overwatering can be just as damaging as underwatering. If compost becomes totally saturated in winter, remove the pot to enable the compost to dry out rapidly. Wrapping several layers of newspaper around the saturated rootball helps to remove excess water.

Fronds become scorched and pale if the plant is in strong sunlight. Remove the plant to indirect light and feed regularly.

Pale, spindly fronds are caused by insufficient food and too dark a position. Move the plant to better light and feed regularly.

PESTS AND DISEASES
Scale insects
Mealy bugs

• Plant Identification p.15 • Propagation by Division p.179 • Ferns pp.186—187 • Pests pp.194—196 • Checklists pp.212—217

GOLDFISH PLANT

Columnea gloriosa
Height: 7.5–13 cm
Spread: 25–45 cm, trailing 60–120 cm

Few trailing plants are more attractive than the goldfish plant, which flowers from early autumn to mid-spring. The long, trailing stems are smothered with small, pale to medium green leaves covered in tiny, reddish hairs. The bright red flowers are tubular, 5–6 cm long and have yellow throats.

C. microphylla has even longer stems, up to 1.5 m in length, with light green leaves covered in purplish hairs. From early winter to mid-spring, it bears a profusion of yellow-throated, orange-red flowers, 4–5 cm long.

C. × banksii, a hybrid of garden origin, has fleshy, dark green leaves on trailing stems, 60–90 cm long. Its vermilion flowers are 6–7.5 cm long, have orange-yellow throats and grow from leaf-joints.

The lipstick vine, *Aeschynanthus radicans*, better known as *A. lobbianus*, needs a slightly lower winter temperature, about 15°C (59°F). Long, trailing shoots bear fleshy, dark green leaves. Bright red, hooded and tubular flowers with creamy-yellow throats appear from mid- to late summer.

The zebra basket vine, *A. marmoratus*, is another trailing plant, with long, waxy, dark green leaves with a lacy network of yellow veins. From June to September, it produces 5 cm-long, tubular, green flowers with chocolate-brown spots.

A. speciosus bears clusters of 7.5 cm-long, tubular, bright orange and yellow flowers with dark lips, that appear from July to September.

All these plants are best grown in indoor hanging baskets, or where the stems can trail unhindered.

COLUMNEA × BANKSII
White berries may follow its vermilion flowers.

COLUMNEA 'MERCUR'
Yellow flowers bloom continuously from spring until late autumn.

◣ SURVIVAL BASICS

Light and temperature: Bright, indirect sunlight; winter temperatures of 13–16°C (55–61°F).

Watering and feeding: Keep compost moist, but not continually saturated. From May to September, add a weak liquid fertilizer every 2–3 weeks.

Compost and repotting: Use John Innes potting compost No. 2, plus sphagnum moss and sharp sand. Repot in summer, every 2 years.

Propagation: In late spring and early summer, take stem-tip cuttings.

WARNING: Winter temperatures below the recommended minimum may prove fatal.

• Plant Identification p.12

COSTA RICA

Leaves soon shrivel in summer if the air is dry and the temperature high. Mist the plant frequently.

Position columneas where the long stems can trail freely. If flowers are accidentally knocked off, plants lose much of their attraction.

Make sure indoor hanging baskets are firmly secured by strong hooks. They are especially heavy after they have been watered.

Columnea gloriosa

PESTS AND DISEASES
Botrytis

• Propagation by Division p.179

• Diseases p.197
• Checklists pp.212–217

S. AMERICA

WANDERING JEW

Tradescantia fluminensis
Height: 7.5–10 cm
Spread: 15–25 cm, trailing 30 cm or more

This popular trailing foliage plant bears a wealth of colourful leaves throughout the year. The fleshy, but stiff, stems have prominent leaf joints that produce pointed, oval leaves 5 cm long. These are bluish-green or dark green on top and pale purple beneath. Common varieties include 'Quicksilver', with silver stripes.
Also recommended:
T. albiflora: Varieties include *T. a.* 'Tricolor' (green leaves striped in white and rose-purple) and *T. a.* 'Aurea' (leaves almost entirely yellow).
Zebrina pendula, the silvery inch plant: Larger leaves, up to 7.5 cm long, medium green with two silvery stripes along the edges. The undersides are purple.

Spindly growth results from inadequate feeding, dry compost or poor light.

SURVIVAL BASICS

Light and temperature: Bright, indirect sunlight; winter temperatures of 7–10°C (45–50°F).
Watering and feeding: Keep compost barely moist in winter. Water freely in summer. In summer, add a weak liquid fertilizer every 2 weeks.
Compost and repotting: Use John Innes potting compost No. 2. Repot, usually every spring, when potbound.
Propagation: Divide and repot congested plants. Alternatively, take stem-tip cuttings 7.5 cm long in spring and summer.

WARNING: Leaves lose their variegations when deprived of light.

Brown and shrivelled leaf tips are caused by dry air or red spider mites.

Yellow, wilted and shrivelled leaves and stems are caused by lack of water.

PESTS AND DISEASES
Red spider mites
Greenfly

• Plant Identification p.16   • Propagation by Cuttings pp.176–178   • Propagation by Division p.179   • Pests pp.194–196   • Checklists pp.212–217

6

SHRIMP PLANT

Justicia brandegeana
Height: 45–60 cm
Spread: 30–45 cm

Few flowering plants are as distinctive as the shrimp plant, often sold as *Beloperone guttata*, which blooms from April to December. Each flower, up to 15 cm long, is formed of overlapping, brown-pink bracts which enclose the white, inconspicuous true flowers.

The structure of the bracts, as well as their colour, is reminiscent of the body of a shrimp — hence the plant's common name. Bracts hang in small clusters from arching stems bearing oval leaves.

To encourage bushy growth, remove all shrimp-like flowers in the first season. Also, for the first two seasons, cut back the new growth by half in spring.

SURVIVAL BASICS

Light and temperature: Bright, indirect sunlight; winter temperatures of 7–10°C (45–50°F).

Watering and feeding: Keep compost barely moist in winter. Water freely in summer, but avoid continual saturation. From April to September, add a weak liquid fertilizer every 2–3 weeks.

Compost and repotting: Use John Innes potting compost No. 2. Repot in spring, when potbound.

Propagation: In spring, take stem-tip cuttings.

WARNING: Avoid high temperatures in winter, when the light is poor, otherwise growth will be weak.

Yellowish bracts
result from insufficient light.

Leaves drop off if the plant is in a cold draught or has not been adequately watered.

Dull coloured leaves and poor flowers
result from lack of food or too much water.

MEXICO

PESTS AND DISEASES
Greenfly
Red spider mites

• Plant Identification p.11   • Propagation by Cuttings pp.176–178   • Pests pp.194–196   • Checklists pp.212–217

BUSY LIZZIE

Impatiens walleriana
Height: 45–60 cm
Spread: 38–45 cm

This popular flowering plant is also sold as *I.sultani*. The compact profusely flowering hybrids are the ones most commonly grown. They produce a wealth of flat, five-petalled flowers in colours including white, orange, pink, purple and red. The hybrids include 'Rose Star' (red flowers crossed with white) and 'Supernova' (pink flowers tinged with red). The 'New Guinea' hybrids, such as 'Fanfare', have multicoloured leaves.

A well-branched relative, *I. petersiana*, grows 38–45 cm high. Throughout summer, it bears 2.5–3 cm-wide, bright red, five-petalled flowers amid burgundy-coloured leaves. Although usually sold as a separate species, it may be classified as *I. walleriana*.

Many varieties are ideal for planting outside in containers during early summer, but some are also suitable for growing in pots indoors in a cool position. These include 'Zig-Zag Mixed' (15 cm high) with striped flowers of orange, rose, pink, salmon and scarlet, on a white background. 'Mini Mixed' (15–20 cm high) has a wide range of colours on branching, but compact, plants. 'Imp Mixed' (15 cm high) has distinctly larger flowers which come in a wide colour range.

'Rosette' (15 cm high) comes in colours including scarlet, rose, salmon, pink and white – and about 25 per cent of the flowers are fully double. 'Sweet Sue' (30 cm high) is larger, with glossy, green leaves and deep orange flowers 6 cm or more wide. 'Starbright' (15 cm high) has large spectacular flowers in a mixture of bright violet, orange, red and rose.

IMPATIENS PETERSIANA
Distinguished by its burgundy-coloured leaves and carmine flowers.

IMPATIENS 'ZIG-ZAG MIXED'
The single, candystripe flowers are white with orange and red.

IMPATIENS 'FANFARE'
The leaves of this New Guinea hybrid are yellow and green, the flowers pink.

SURVIVAL BASICS

Light and temperature: Bright, indirect sunlight, especially in summer; winter temperature, 10°C (50°F).

Watering and feeding: Keep compost damp in winter, watering freely in summer. Do not let the compost become waterlogged. From May to September, add a weak liquid fertilizer every 7–10 days.

Compost and repotting: Use John Innes potting compost No. 2, or a peat-based mix.

Propagation: Take 10 cm-long stem-tip cuttings in summer.

WARNING: Low temperatures and cold draughts in winter cause leaves to wilt, turn yellow and fall.

E. AFRICA

Flowers may not appear on mature plants that have been recently repotted. Busy lizzies flower best when potbound.

Poor flowering results from poor light, lack of food, overfeeding, or too low a temperature.

Leaves and stems wilt if the mix is too wet or too dry. Check and rectify. The plant will need a lot of water during summer, so check the compost every day.

Spindly growth, especially in winter, results from too little light and too much warmth.

Impatiens walleriana

PESTS AND DISEASES
Red spider mites
Greenfly

• Propagation by Cuttings pp.176–178

• Pests pp.194–196
• Checklists pp.212–217

ALUMINIUM PLANT

Pilea cadierei
Height: 25–30 cm
Spread: 20–25 cm

This popular bushy foliage plant has oval, leathery, dark green, slightly-quilted leaves with silvery splashes between the veins. The smaller type, *P. c.* 'Nana', grows to 23 cm high, and is small enough to be planted in a bottle garden.

The artillery plant or gunpowder plant, *P. microphylla*, is much branched and bushy, growing 23 cm high and 15–20 cm wide. The stems bear flattened sprays of pale to medium green leaves with a feathery appearance. From May to September, it produces yellow-green flowers which, when mature, puff out tiny clouds of pollen – hence its common name.

SURVIVAL BASICS

Light and temperature: Bright, indirect sunlight or light shade; winter temperatures of 10–13°C (50–55°F).
Watering and feeding: Keep compost barely moist in winter, but water freely in summer. Avoid continual saturation. From April to September, add a weak liquid fertilizer every 2–3 weeks.
Compost and repotting: Use John Innes potting compost No. 2. Repot in spring, when potbound.
Propagation: In late spring, take 7.5–10 cm stem-tip cuttings.

WARNING: Do not overwater in winter, as the leaves will lose their colour, wilt and fall.

Pale, spindly growth results from insufficient food and poor light. Feed the plant and place it in better light.

Leaves will fall in winter if the plant is in a cold draught.

VIETNAM

PESTS AND DISEASES
Mealy bugs
Greenfly

• Plant Identification p.26   • Propagation by Cuttings pp.176–178   • Pests pp.194–196   • Checklists pp.212–217

CHENILLE PLANT

Acalypha hispida
Height: 0.9–1.2 m
Spread: 30–45 cm

This beautiful plant produces long, drooping tassles, resembling soft embroidery fringes, during summer and early autumn. They may reach 38 cm in length and are formed of hundreds of small, bright scarlet flowers. The oval, bright green leaves are slightly hairy, 12.5–20 cm long and 7.5 cm wide. Varieties with green or cream tassles are also available.

As the tassles fade and die, cut them off. This helps to tidy up the plant in winter. In spring, cut back by half all the growth made during the previous year and use the cuttings to propagate new plants. Plants do not flower until they are about one year old.

Red spider mites are the worst enemy, especially if the atmosphere is dry. These small, spider-like creatures spin webs, mainly on the undersides of the leaves. Use an insecticide, mist the leaves and keep the compost moist.

Remove flowers as soon as they start to lose colour. This encourages the development of further tassles.

PESTS AND DISEASES
Red spider mites
Greenfly

SURVIVAL BASICS

Light and temperature: Bright, indirect sunlight; winter temperature of 15°C (59°F).
Watering and feeding: Keep compost just moist in winter. Water freely in summer, especially when in flower. From late spring to autumn, add a weak liquid fertilizer every 10–14 days.
Compost and repotting: Use John Innes potting compost No. 2 for large plants; small ones grow well in a peat-based mix. Repot in spring.
Propagation: By stem-tip cuttings, 10 cm long, in spring.

WARNING: Dry, cold air in winter will make the leaves fall off.

• Plant Identification p.11   • Propagation by Cuttings pp.176–178   • Pests pp.194–196   • Checklists pp.212–217

INDIAN AZALEA

Rhododendron simsii
Height: 30–45 cm
Spread: 38–45 cm

DOUBLE
Rhododendron simsii
hybrid

This profusely ᵊflowering, bushy, semi-evergreen plant is a popular gift at Christmas. It is usually bought when the flower buds are just beginning to show colour, and remains in bloom for several weeks.

SINGLE
Rhododendron hybrid

There are many attractive varieties, each with 5–7.5 cm-wide, funnel-shaped flowers, in shades of red, orange, pink and white, as well as multicoloured. They may be single or double and some are frilly-edged.

Outdoors, azaleas usually flower in spring, but professional growers, by manipulating temperatures and active growth periods, can produce a succession of plants that flower indoors from early winter through to spring.

FRILLY-EDGED
Rhododendron simsii
hybrid

Only buy those plants that have colour showing in their buds, are of an even shape and have a moist compost. Do not buy plants that have been left standing outside florists in cold, draughty conditions. The buds will fall when the plants are taken indoors and exposed to higher temperatures.

Some nurserymen remove many of the buds, so that fewer but larger flowers are produced. If this has been done, do not try to keep the plant for another year.

Plants that have not been disbudded can be planted outside in spring, if the site is not too exposed or continually subjected to low temperatures, especially in late winter and early spring. Set the plant in a peaty, moisture-retentive soil outdoors. Add bonemeal to the soil to encourage rapid root development. Do not be disappointed if your azalea fails to flower well in its first season after being planted out.

SURVIVAL BASICS

Light and temperature: Shaded sunlight; winter temperatures of 10–15°C (50–59°F).

Watering and potting: When in flower, keep compost moist, but never waterlogged. From the time the plant is bought and the buds show colour, feed every 2 weeks with a weak liquid fertilizer.

Compost and repotting: Use a lime-free, peaty mix such as equal parts John Innes potting compost No. 2 and peat compost.

Propagation: From stem-tip cuttings of new growth in spring.

WARNING: High temperatures and dry compost spell disaster.

• Plant Identification p.11

Keep the compost moist at all times. To make sure of this, immerse the pot up to its neck and leave it until the surface of the compost glistens. Afterward, drain it thoroughly.

Flowers will last for many weeks when the plant is kept in a cool room.

Falling buds and undeveloped flowers may be due to cold draughts. Dry compost can have the same effect.

Yellow leaves result from lime in the compost or from water with a high alkaline content. Use rainwater, or apply iron-based compounds to counteract the lime.

Rhododendron simsii

PESTS AND DISEASES
Leaf miners

• Pests pp.194–196
• Checklists pp.212–217

PAINTED NET LEAF

Fittonia verschaffeltii
Height: 7.5–5 cm
Spread: trailing and creeping

This unusual, sprawling, foliage plant bears oval, dark green leaves up to 13 cm long, with veins distinctively lined in carmine-pink.

F. v. 'Argyroneura' has a more delicate appearance. The 10 cm-long leaves have veins daintily lined in ivory-white. This has led to its many common names: nerve plant, silver net leaf, lace leaf, and snakeskin plant. It needs slightly higher temperatures than *F. verschaffeltii*, that is, not less than 16°C (61°F) in winter.

The dwarf form, *F. v.* 'Nana', has been recently introduced as a houseplant and is easier to grow. Its leaves are 2.5 cm long with white veins.

SURVIVAL BASICS

Light and temperature: Bright, indirect sunlight in winter, shaded in summer; winter temperature of 13°C (55°F).

Watering and feeding: Keep compost barely moist in winter. Water freely in summer. From April to September, add a weak liquid fertilizer every 2 weeks.

Compost and repotting: Use John Innes potting compost No. 2, or a peat-based mix. Repot in spring.

Propagation: Divide congested plants in spring.

WARNING: Low temperatures and waterlogged compost in winter will kill the plant.

Yellow, wilting leaves in summer are usually due to waterlogged compost. Remove the pot to enable rapid drying.

Wrapping several layers of newspaper around the rootball helps to remove excess water.

Shrivelled leaves result from a dry atmosphere and from standing in strong sunlight.

PESTS AND DISEASES
Greenfly

• Plant Identification p.15   • Propagation by Division p.179   • Pests pp.194–196   • Checklists pp.212–217

7

FLAMING KATY

Kalanchoe blossfeldiana
Height: 20–30 cm
Spread: 20–25 cm

This bushy succulent is sold in flower throughout the year. Its natural flowering time is late winter to late spring, but by manipulating the amount of darkness it is given, professional growers can induce it to flower at any time.

The tubular, scarlet, 12–25 mm-long flowers are borne in dense heads. Red, pink, white or yellow varieties are also available.

Also recommended:
K. daigremontiana, the Mexican hat plant: Better known as *Bryophyllum daigremontianum*. Upright, about 90 cm high, with large, fleshy leaves that bear a row of plantlets at their edges.

SURVIVAL BASICS

Light and temperature: Bright, indirect sunlight; winter temperature of 10°C (50°F).
Watering and feeding: In winter, keep compost slightly moist, but water freely in summer. Allow compost to dry out between waterings. Add a weak liquid fertilizer every 3–4 weeks in summer.
Compost and repotting: Use John Innes potting compost No. 2. Old leggy plants can be discarded after flowering; repot young ones.
Propagation: By stem-tip cuttings in spring.

WARNING: Never use pesticide sprays containing malathion.

After flowering, the plants are best discarded and fresh ones bought.

Do not mist the leaves – they soon look unsightly if water repeatedly falls on them.

Roots rapidly rot if the plant is excessively watered, especially in winter. If in doubt about watering, err on the dry side.

PESTS AND DISEASES
Mealy bugs

• Plant Identification p.11   • Pests pp.194–196
• Checklists pp.212–217

HOT WATER PLANT

Achimenes grandiflora
Height: 45–60 cm
Spread: 38–45 cm

In summer, this bushy glossy-leaved relative of the African violet is smothered with large, flat, purplish-red flowers that are about 5 cm wide. If you want a bushy plant, nip out the ends of the shoots to encourage each of them to divide. If you are growing achimenes in a hanging basket, do not nip out the shoots.

A. *longiflora* also looks at its best in a hanging basket. The sprawling stems reach about 30 cm long and, from July to September, bear flowers in colours from pale red to purple-blue. Each flower is about 5 cm wide and rises singly from a leaf joint.

There are several excellent varieties, such as 'Major', with a metallic sheen to the green leaves, and violet-blue flowers 7.5 cm wide with golden-yellow throats. The form 'Alba' has white flowers of the same size with yellow throats that are spotted purple.

There are also many hybrids, raised by crossing different species to produce a broad colour range, and these can be ordered from nursery catalogues.

These plants gained their common name from the erroneous belief of early gardeners that they needed hot water during their early stages to induce growth. However, the rhizomes do benefit from slightly tepid water.

Achimenes grow from small rhizomes that can be bought in late winter. Buy only those that are plump and fresh. Plant six to eight of them, 2.5 cm deep, in a 15 cm pot. Water with tepid water and keep at 15°C (59°F). This is an easier, more reliable and quicker way to produce plants than by sowing seeds.

ACHIMENES HYBRID
The blooms can be red, white, blue, pink, purple, yellow or bicoloured.

ACHIMENES 'ENGLISH WALTZ'
Distinguished by its dark green leaves and pink flowers with yellow throats.

SURVIVAL BASICS

Light and temperature: Bright, indirect sunlight; winter temperature of 15°C (59°F).

Watering and feeding: Until early spring, water sparingly, but increase the amount as the plant grows. From April to July, add a weak liquid fertilizer every 2 weeks. After July, use a high potash fertilizer.

Compost and repotting: Use John Innes potting compost No. 2. Repot each year, in late winter.

Propagation: Plant rhizomes in late winter.

WARNING: Never let the compost dry out when the plants are in flower, or the blooms will fall.

Wilting foliage and stems result from either too much or too little water. Check the compost. If it is totally saturated, remove the pot for a day or so. Wrapping several layers of newspaper around the rootball helps to absorb excess water.

If the plant fails to flower or produces brown buds, it may have been exposed to too high temperatures. Prolonged exposure to strong sunlight will have the same effect.

Dry air encourages red spider mites to attack the plant. To deter these pests, occasionally mist around the base of the plant with tepid water. Take care not to wet the leaves.

Achimenes longiflora

PESTS AND DISEASES
Red spider mites

• Pests pp.194–196
• Checklists pp.212–217

PERSIAN VIOLET

Exacum affine
Height: 15—25 cm
Spread: 15—25 cm

This bushy flowering plant is best bought when the buds are just showing colour. Its common names indicate some confusion about its origin: in North America, for example, it is also known as the German violet. In fact it comes from the Island of Socotra in the Indian Ocean.

From July to September, its fragrant, saucer-shaped flowers which are lavender-blue with bright yellow centres and 12—18 mm wide, rise above the shining, deep green leaves.

The violet is really a perennial, although plants are best bought each year and treated as annuals. They are usually discarded after flowering.

SURVIVAL BASICS

Light and temperature: Bright, indirect sunlight; winter temperatures of 13—16°C (55—61°F).
Watering and feeding: Keep compost moist but not saturated. When in flower, add a weak liquid fertilizer every 7—10 days.
Compost and repotting: Use John Innes potting compost No. 2, but repotting is unnecessary as plants are discarded after flowering.
Propagation: Buy new plants in midsummer or sow seeds in spring.

WARNING: Do not buy a plant in full flower, but select one with plenty of buds.

Poor flowering results if faded and dead flowers are left on the plant. Pinching out prolongs the flowering period and prevents the plant's energies being directed into the development of seed.

Hot temperatures in summer shorten the flowering period.

Is. of SOCOTRA

After flowering, plants are best discarded and fresh ones bought the following year.

Wilting, caused by lack of water, hinders blooming by preventing the development of unopened flowers. Never let the compost dry out, whatever the time of year.

PESTS AND DISEASES
Greenfly

• Plant Identification p.10   • Checklists pp.212—217
• Pests pp.194—196

POLKA DOT PLANT

Hypoestes phyllostachya
Height: 45–60 cm
Spread: 30–45 cm

This small, shrubby plant is suitably described by its common name. The olive-green, oval leaves are speckled with white to pinkish spots and blotches.

The plant naturally sprawls, but shoots can be nipped back to encourage bushy, upright growth. Alternatively, set the plant in a hanging basket and allow the stems to spread and trail. Small lavender flowers appear in summer. Nip these out to encourage better leaf colour.

Also recommended:
H. aristata, the ribbon bush: Upright, rounded shrub. Oval, medium green leaves are crowned with spikes of mauve flowers in summer.

SURVIVAL BASICS

Light and temperature: Bright light, with some direct sunlight; winter temperature of 15°C (59°F).
Watering and feeding: In winter, keep compost just moist, but water freely in summer. In summer, add a weak liquid fertilizer every 2–3 weeks.
Compost and repotting: Use John Innes potting compost No. 2. Repot when potbound; leggy, large plants are best discarded.
Propagation: Take stem-tip cuttings in spring or early summer.

WARNING: In poor light, leaves lose their attractive markings and turn green.

Wilting leaves indicate that the potting mix is either too wet or too dry. Check and rectify.

Yellow, wilting leaves result if the plant is in a cold draught.

MADAGASCAR

PESTS AND DISEASES
Mealy bugs
Scale insects
Greenfly
Whitefly

• Plant Identification p.27   • Propagation by Cuttings pp.176–178   • Pests pp.194–196   • Checklists pp.212–217

AFRICAN VIOLET

Saintpaulia ionantha
Height: 7.5–13 cm
Spread: 15–23 cm

Few flowering plants can compete in popularity with this East African native from the coastal region of Tanzania. Its attractions include velvety leaves and brilliantly coloured flowers.

When first introduced to Europe and America as a houseplant in the 1920s, it was difficult to grow. Since then, however, numerous tougher and freer-flowering forms have been bred and raised. These bloom throughout the year.

African violets are best grown on shaded, draught-free windowsills. They also thrive in kitchens and bathrooms, where warmth is coupled with high humidity.

In dark rooms, these plants can be ideal subjects for growing in artificial light. Use two 40-watt fluorescent tubes, suspended 30–38 cm above the plants, and switch them on for 12 hours a day. Do not use the normal tungsten-filament bulbs: these do not emit light that encourages growth.

The 'normal' type of African violet bears single, five-petalled, violet-purple flowers, 15–18 mm wide, in clusters of two to eight on stalks up to 13 cm long. Each flower has a small, but conspicuous, yellow pollen sac which stands out brightly like a golden eye.

Saintpaulia hybrids are widely grown, and there are hundreds of varieties to choose from, all of which thrive indoors. 'Ballet' and 'Melodie' hybrids are particularly easy to grow. Colours range from white, through shades of pink, carmine and red to mauve, purple and blue. Bicoloured flowers are also readily available. Mature hybrid plants may have a spread of 16–30 cm.

DOUBLE
Flowers with twice, or more, the normal number of petals.
Variety illustrated:
'Top Job'

BICOLOURED
Petals are in two colours, either contrasting, or in two shades of the same colour.
Variety illustrated:
'Confusa'

FRINGED
Petals are frilled or fringed at the edges.
Variety illustrated:
'Fancy Pants'

SURVIVAL BASICS

Light and temperature: Bright, indirect sunlight; winter temperature of 13°C (55°F).

Watering and feeding: Keep compost moist but not constantly saturated. From May to September, add a weak liquid fertilizer every 2–3 weeks. Feed monthly in winter.

Compost and repotting: Use a lime-free, peat-based mix and small containers to a final size of 15 cm wide. Repot in spring.

Propagation: Take leaf-stem cuttings from June to September.

WARNING: Some pesticides will damage saintpaulias, so always check the label before use.

Mottled, discoloured leaves result from greenfly attacks. Use an artist's brush to remove them. Treat severe attacks by chemical means.

Discoloured petals are due to direct sunlight.

Yellow rings form on foliage splashed with water. Always water from below, through a saucer.

Poor flowering is caused by inadequate or irregular feeding, too low a temperature or too little light in winter.

Shrivelled, yellow leaves result from low temperatures and high humidity. In cold rooms, help prevent this by reducing the frequency of watering. Alternatively, move to a warmer room.

Mealy bugs often infest leaf joints and the crowns of plants. Treat with an insecticide. Black mould may follow mealy bug attack. Wipe it off with cotton wool soaked in methylated spirits.

Saintpaulia ionantha

Roots will rot if the compost is continually wet.

PESTS AND DISEASES
Greenfly
Mealy bugs
Black mould

• Propagation by
  Cuttings pp.176–178

• Pests pp.194–196
• Diseases p.197

• Checklists pp.212–217

EMERALD RIPPLE

Peperomia caperata
Height: 10–25 cm
Spread: 13–15 cm

This easy-to-grow, bushy foliage plant boasts a mass of deeply-corrugated, dark green, glistening leaves on red or pink stems. From April to December, it bears unusual, white, poker-like flower spikes.

The desert privet, *P. magnoliifolia*, is more branched and shrubby. The true species, with its thick, fleshy, glossy, green leaves, is less popular than the variegated forms: 'Variegata' (cream-coloured when young, later cream and light green) and 'Green Gold' (cream edges to large, light green leaves).

Also recommended:
P. griseoargentea, the silver ripple: Heart-shaped leaves have a silvery shimmer.

SURVIVAL BASICS

Light and temperature: Bright, indirect sunlight; winter temperatures of 13–15°C (55–59°).

Watering and feeding: In winter, water sparingly; water more in summer, but let the compost dry out first. From May to September, add a weak liquid fertilizer every 2 weeks.

Compost and repotting: Use John Innes potting compost No. 1, or a peat-based type. Repot in spring, when potbound.

Propagation: Take stem-tip or leaf-stem cuttings in spring or early summer.

WARNING: Avoid low temperatures and wet compost in winter.

TROPICAL AMERICA

Brown tips and edges to leaves result from sudden drops in temperature. Avoid draughts from doors and windows.

Leaves will wilt if the compost is too wet or too dry. If too wet, remove the pot to allow air to dry out the compost. If too dry, apply water before the leaves wilt badly, but make sure the potting mix is not continually wet.

PESTS AND DISEASES
Mealy bugs
Red spider mites
Greenfly

• Plant Identification p.27   • Propagation by Cuttings pp.176–178   • Pests pp.194–196   • Checklists pp.212–217

CORAL BERRY

Ardisia crenata
Height: 60–90 cm
Spread: 30–45 cm

This slow-growing, upright, evergreen looks best as one of a group of floor-standing plants. The deep green, shiny, wavy-edged leaves are up to 10 cm long. In late May and into June it produces 12 mm-wide, sweetly-scented, cream-white, star-shaped flowers, sometimes tinged pink. To encourage these blooms, water the plant well.

The flowers are followed by large clusters of round, scarlet berries that sometimes remain on the plant until the following year. In fact, the fruiting season is so long that plants can have berries on low branches, with a profusion of white flowers above.

SURVIVAL BASICS

Light and temperature: Bright, but indirect sunlight; winter temperatures of 7–10°C (45–50°F).
Watering and feeding: In winter, keep compost barely moist. Water freely in summer, never letting the compost dry out. From April to September, add a weak liquid fertilizer every week.
Compost and repotting: Use John Innes potting compost No. 2. Repot in spring, when potbound, usually every 3–4 years.
Propagation: Take 7.5 cm-long stem cuttings in summer.

WARNING: Never let the compost dry out, especially in summer.

E. INDIES

Leggy plants, with just a few leaves at their tops, can be rejuvenated by cutting back the main stem to within 7.5–10 cm of the base in early spring.

If pests become a problem, apply a systemic insecticide to the compost so that the entire plant becomes toxic to insects.

As a slow-growing, floor-standing plant, it needs a position protected from children and large dogs if it is to survive.

PESTS AND DISEASES
Greenfly
Mealy bugs

• Plant Identification p.31   • Propagation by
                                   Cuttings pp.176–178   • Pests pp.194–196
                                                            • Checklists pp.212–217

PRAYER PLANT

Maranta leuconeura
Height: 15–20 cm
Spread: 25–30 cm

This bushy, compact, low-growing plant has strikingly marked, oval to oblong leaves. They are emerald-green with light brown or dark green blotches between the veins. With age, they turn grey and the blotches darken.

The plant's common name comes from the leaves' habit of folding at night, as if in prayer. Several forms are widely grown, including rabbit tracks, *M. l. kerchoveana*. This has light green leaves with characteristic brown patches between the veins which, as the name suggests, resemble a rabbit's footprint.

The herringbone plant, *M. l. tricolor*, also known as *M. l. erythrophylla*, has deep olive-green leaves with greyish-green edges, striking red veins and bright green, irregular markings along the midrib.

M. l. massangeana, often known as *M. l. leuconeura*, is smaller than the herringbone plant. Its leaves are blackish-green with silver markings either side of the midrib, silver veins and pale green edges.

Many marantas are now classified as *Calathea*, although some nurseries still sell the peacock plant, *Calathea makoyana*, as *Maranta makoyana* (see p. 88).

The never never plant was formerly classified as a *Maranta* but is now called *Ctenanthe oppenheimiana*. Its spear-shaped leaves often reach 38 cm in length. They have a velvety surface boldly contrasted in light and dark green. The undersides are purple. The form *C. o. tricolor* has leaves blotched with cream. It does well in shady conditions, but in strong sunlight its leaves will curl.

MARANTA LEUCONEURA
KERCHOVEANA
The dominant brown patches on the leaves darken with age.

MARANTA LEUCONEURA
MASSANGEANA
The blackish-green leaves have distinctive silvery markings and veins.

SURVIVAL BASICS

Light and temperature: Light shade, away from bright sunlight; winter temperatures of 10–13°C (50–55°F).

Watering and feeding: Keep compost slightly moist in winter; water freely in summer. From May to September, add a weak liquid fertilizer every 2–3 weeks.

Compost and repotting: Use John Innes potting compost No. 2 or a peat-based type. Repot in spring.

Propagation: Divide congested plants in spring.

WARNING: Warmth in winter is essential to prevent leaves turning brown and shrivelling.

Lower leaves turn yellow or curl when the compost dries out. During the active growth period, keep the compost moist at all times.

Brown leaf tips and wilting leaves result from dry air. Mist the leaves frequently. A damp atmosphere also helps to deter red spider mites.

Leaves become bleached if exposed to direct sunlight, especially in summer.

Maranta leuconeura erythrophylla

PESTS AND DISEASES
Red spider mites
Mealy bugs

• Propagation by Division p.179

• Pests pp.194–196
• Checklists pp.212–217

PEACOCK PLANT

Calathea makoyana
Height: 45–60 cm
Spread: 30–45 cm

This bushy plant has 15 cm-long, oval leaves which are silvery-green with medium green edges and irregularly marked with dark green splashes. The undersides are marked with reddish-purple splashes.

The zebra plant, *C. zebrina*, has oblong leaves which are semi-erect, splayed outward and up to 45 cm long. The soft, emerald-green background is veined in pale green with bright green strips between the veins.

The rattlesnake plant, *C. insignis*, has upright, wavy-edged, yellowish leaves with large and small, dark green patches and rich maroon undersides.

SURVIVAL BASICS

Light and temperature: Light shade, away from strong sunlight; winter temperatures of 15–18°C (59–64°F).

Watering and feeding: Keep compost moist in winter, but water freely in summer. From April to September, add a weak liquid fertilizer every 2 weeks.

Compost and repotting: Use John Innes potting compost No. 2. Repot in spring, every other year.

Propagation: Divide when plants outgrow their pots.

WARNING: Low temperatures, cold draughts and saturated compost in winter are fatal.

Discoloured and scorched leaves result when the plant is placed in strong sunlight. Move to shade immediately.

Yellowish leaves, curling at the edges, are caused by a dry compost. Eventually, unless the plant is watered, the leaves will turn brown and the plant will die.

Leaves fall off if the air is dry. Mist the foliage daily. This also helps to deter red spider mites.

BRAZIL

PESTS AND DISEASES
Red spider mites

• Plant Identification p.26   • Propagation by Division p.179   • Pests pp.194–196   • Checklists pp.212–217

DUMB CANE

Dieffenbachia maculata
Height: 0.45–1.2 m
Spread: 30–45 cm

The leaves of this widely grown foliage plant are long, spear-shaped, glossy and dark green, with large creamy-white splashes between the veins.

The several beautiful forms include 'Exotica', with leaves almost totally creamy-yellow and narrow, pale green edges. 'Splendens' has rich bronze-green leaves, with irregular, small, creamy-white and ivory splashes.

D. amoena eventually forms a trunk-like stem bearing large, 30 cm-wide, 45 cm-long, deep green leaves with creamy-white bands and mottling. The variety 'Tropic Snow' has pale green and cream variegations.

SURVIVAL BASICS

Light and temperature: Bright, indirect sunlight; winter temperatures of 15–18°C (59–64°F).

Watering and feeding: Keep compost barely moist in winter; water freely in summer. From April to September, add a weak liquid fertilizer every 10–14 days.

Compost and repotting: Use John Innes potting compost No. 2 or 3. Repot annually, in spring.

Propagation: Take stem cuttings in spring.

WARNING: The sap is poisonous. Keep the plant away from small children and animals. Wear rubber gloves when handling.

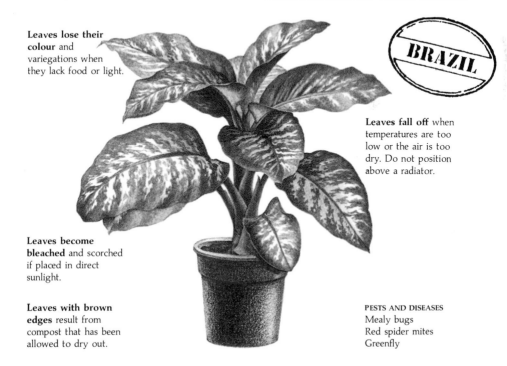

Leaves lose their colour and variegations when they lack food or light.

BRAZIL

Leaves fall off when temperatures are too low or the air is too dry. Do not position above a radiator.

Leaves become bleached and scorched if placed in direct sunlight.

Leaves with brown edges result from compost that has been allowed to dry out.

PESTS AND DISEASES
Mealy bugs
Red spider mites
Greenfly

• Plant Identification p.27 • Propagation by Cuttings p.181 • Pests pp.194–196 • Checklists pp.212–217

PAINTER'S PALETTE

Anthurium andreanum
Height: 38—45 cm
Spread: 30 cm

The waxy, red, heart-shaped spathe forms a distinctive 'collar' 10 cm long and 7.5 cm wide. From the centre of this spathe rises an arched spire or spadix 7.5 cm long, formed of minute white or yellow flowers. The dark green, heart-shaped leaves are up to 20 cm long and borne on wiry stems. The flowers appear from May to September. The 'Album' variety has white spathes.

The flamingo plant, *A. scherzerianum*, is smaller, at 23—30 cm high and 30—38 cm wide. The dark green, lance-shaped leaves grow up to 18 cm long. From April to October, it produces brilliant scarlet spathes from which rise long, golden-yellow spires that curve in a manner reminiscent of a flamingo's neck.

The crystal anthurium, *A. crystallinum*, though not easy to grow, is one of the most attractive of all foliage houseplants. It grows to about 45 cm high and 30—38 cm wide, and bears soft, velvety, emerald-green, heart-shaped leaves up to 60 cm long and 30 cm wide. Their veins and midribs are picked out in ivory and look pale pink from beneath. From May to September, it produces insignificant green flowers.

The king anthurium, *A. veitchii*, grows up to 90 cm high. Its large, bluish-green, quilted leaves may reach as much as 75 cm in length.

The queen anthurium, *A. warocqueanum*, also has large, velvety leaves, up to 75 cm in length. They are green with ivory-white veins. Anthuriums with large leaves must be placed where they cannot be damaged, for once torn they lose much of their glamour.

ANTHURIUM SCHERZERIANUM
The spathe may be bright scarlet, pink or dark red with white spots.

ANTHURIUM CRYSTALLINUM
The decorative leaves are metallic-purple when young, later turning to bright emerald-green.

SURVIVAL BASICS

Light and temperature: Bright, indirect sunlight; winter temperatures of 15—18°C (59—64°F).

Watering and feeding: Keep compost barely moist in winter; water freely in summer. From April to September, add a weak liquid fertilizer every 10 days.

Compost and repotting: Use equal parts peat-based compost and sphagnum moss. Repot in spring, when potbound.

Propagation: Divide and repot congested plants.

WARNING: Draughts and low temperatures in winter can be fatal, especially if the compost is kept wet.

• Plant Identification p.9

COLOMBIA

Mist the plant daily to prevent flower heads shrivelling, but shield them from the spray.

Lack of flowers is due to inadequate feeding. Encourage growth by feeding regularly.

Yellow edges on the leaves are due to cold draughts or dry air.

Remove dust from the leaves of flowering anthuriums with a damp sponge. But clean the delicate leaves of *A. crystallinum* by regular misting.

Support tall flower stalks by tying them to thin canes.

Anthurium andreanum

PESTS AND DISEASES
Mealy bugs
Greenfly

• Propagation by Division p.179

• Pests pp.194–196
• Checklists pp.212–217

CHINESE EVERGREEN

Aglaonema treubii
Height: 15–23 cm
Spread: 23–30 cm

This evergreen houseplant has grey-green leaves with silvery-grey blotches. It also bears white, arum-like flowers 5 cm long during July; these are followed by dark red berries.

A. *modestum* is grown for its lance-shaped, waxy, green leaves which are flecked with silvery-grey. It is much larger, growing 45–75 cm high and 45–60 cm wide. The form 'Silver Queen' has grey-green leaves mottled and patched in silvery greyish-green.

Also recommended:

A. *pseudobracteatum*, the white rajah or golden evergreen: Spear-shaped, rich green leaves have creamy-gold splashes.

SURVIVAL BASICS

Light and temperature: Diffused light, not direct sunlight; winter temperatures of 15–18°C (59–64°F).

Watering and feeding: Keep compost just moist in winter, water freely in summer. From April to September, add a weak liquid fertilizer every 2 weeks.

Compost and repotting: Use John Innes potting compost No. 2, or a peat-based type. Repot in spring, about every 3–4 years.

Propagation: Divide and repot congested plants.

WARNING: Warmth and moist air are essential. Keep away from draughts and smoky air.

Scorched, curled leaves result from strong sunlight.

E. INDIES

Curled, brown leaf edges result from cold draughts.

Brown, shrivelled leaf tips are caused by dry air, so mist the plant frequently.

Wilting leaves indicate too much or too little moisture. If the compost is soaked, remove the pot to allow air to dry off the rootball.

PESTS AND DISEASES
Red spider mites
Mealy bugs

• Plant Identification p.27   • Propagation by Division p.179   • Pests pp.194–196
• Checklists pp.212–217

CAST IRON PLANT

Aspidistra elatior
Height: 30–38 cm
Spread: 38–50 cm

Few houseplants are as well known as this one. Its spear-shaped leaves are 38–50 cm long and grow on short, stiff stems. When they first appear, the leaves are a bright, fresh green; with age, they become shiny and blackish-green.

A variegated form, *A.e.* 'Variegata', has green leaves with white or cream stripes of varying widths. *A.e.* 'Maculata' has blackish-green leaves with white spots.

Aspidistras were popular in Victorian times largely because their 'cast iron' constitution enabled them to survive in smoke-filled parlours and saloons, or in rooms that were almost invariably cold. Today, they flourish in clean air, good light and warmth.

Brown marks on leaves are due to a constantly saturated compost.

Leaves split if the plant is fed too often. Stop feeding the plant for a few months, then use a very weak fertilizer solution.

Dirty leaves are best cleaned with a soft, damp cloth.

Scorched leaves result from strong sunlight, so place in a shaded position.

SURVIVAL BASICS

Light and temperature: Bright, indirect sunlight; winter temperatures of 7–10°C (45–50°F).
Watering and feeding: Keep compost barely moist in winter. Water freely in summer, but do not keep compost saturated. From April to September, add a weak liquid fertilizer every 3–4 weeks.
Compost and repotting: Use John Innes potting compost No. 2 or 3. Repot in spring, every 4–5 years, when potbound.
Propagation: Divide and repot congested plants.

WARNING: Do not allow the compost to remain saturated.

PESTS AND DISEASES
Red spider mites
Scale insects

HYDRANGEA

Hydrangea macrophylla
Height: 30–60 cm
Spread: 30–45 cm

The large, many-flowered heads of this deciduous shrub make an attractive and impressive indoor display. Colours include blue, pink, white, purple and red.

There are two kinds of hydrangea. The hortensia types, commonly known as mop-heads, have large, round, showy heads 15–20 cm wide and are the kind usually grown indoors. The lacecaps have more open, flat heads, 10–15 cm across and are mainly grown outdoors.

Hydrangeas will flower outdoors in temperate climates from July to September, but they can be induced to flower indoors in late spring and early summer.

The degree of alkalinity or acidity of the compost has an influence on flower colour. Blue varieties will produce good, blue flowers when grown in acid compost. Even pink varieties tend to become blue in acid compost. Some growers deliberately 'blue' pink varieties by growing them in acid conditions and adding a proprietary 'blueing' compound to the water just before the flowers open. Similarly, blue varieties turn pink in alkaline compost.

In late September, when the plant loses its leaves, prune the shoots to leave a pair of strong buds on that season's new wood. At the same time, repot it. Plants in 20-cm pots can be repotted in pots of the same size; smaller plants can be repotted in pots one size larger.

Water the compost and place the plant in a cool, frostproof position. In late January, slowly introduce it to a brighter, warmer spot, initially 7–10°C (45–50°F) increasing to 13°C (55°F), but no higher. Keep the compost moist, but water freely when leaves appear.

HORTENSIA
Hydrangea macrophylla hybrid

HORTENSIA
Hydrangea macrophylla hybrid

HORTENSIA
Hydrangea macrophylla
'Générale Vicomtesse de Vibraye'

SURVIVAL BASICS

Light and temperature: Bright, indirect sun; for temperatures, see text.
Watering and feeding: While the plant is in flower, keep the compost moist at all times. Give less water when blooming is over. From when the buds are formed, and until midsummer, add a weak liquid fertilizer every week.
Compost and repotting: Use John Innes potting compost No. 2 or 3. Repot in late summer.
Propagation: Buy young plants.

WARNING: Temperatures above 13°C (55°F) shorten the flowering period and may even cause the plant to collapse.

• Plant Identification p.9

Do not buy plants that have all of their flowers wide open — they will not provide a long display. Instead choose one with large, plump buds. Buy in spring and avoid those with weak and straggly stems or with only a few leaves. Good plants should remain in flower for about 6 weeks.

The plant will collapse if the compost dries out. In this event, soak the rootball in water for an hour. Even if the remedy works, the revived plant will have a shortened flowering period.

Yellowing foliage and poor flower colour (in blue varieties) are due to a compost that is too alkaline. Use rainwater in areas where the tapwater is hard and limy.

JAPAN CHINA

Brown leaf edges indicate that the compost has dried out. Always keep it moist — check the plant daily, especially when it is in full flower.

Hydrangea macrophylla

PESTS AND DISEASES
Red spider mites
Greenfly

• Pests pp.194–196
• Checklists pp.212–217

DRAGON TREE

Dracaena deremensis
Height: 0.75–1.2 m
Spread: 38–45 cm

This evergreen, palm-like plant has narrow, pointed leaves that grow up to 38 cm long in mature plants. They are dark green with pendulous tips and a whitish-green midrib.

Two varieties are particularly popular for their striking foliage. 'Bausei' has 5 cm-wide, 45 cm-long, dark green leaves with a broad, white central stripe. 'Warneckii' has dark green leaves with two white stripes (see illustration).

Also recommended:

D. sanderiana, the ribbon plant: Deep green, slightly wavy-edged leaves are 20 cm long with white or silvery edges.

Brown tips and yellow edges to the leaves are caused by a dry atmosphere or cold draughts.

Bleached and dry patches on the leaves are caused by strong sunlight.

Wilting leaves that fall prematurely are caused by too much or too little water. Remove an overwatered plant from the pot to enable the compost to dry out. Soak a dried out plant for an hour or two.

Brown tips and spots on the leaves indicate dry compost.

PESTS AND DISEASES
Scale insects
Mealy bugs

SURVIVAL BASICS

Light and temperature: Bright, indirect sunlight; winter temperature of 13°C (55°F).

Watering and feeding: Keep the compost just moist in winter; water freely in summer. From April to September, add a weak liquid fertilizer every 2 weeks.

Compost and repotting: Use John Innes potting compost No. 2 or 3. Repot in spring, usually every 2 years.

Propagation: Take 7.5-cm stem cuttings in spring.

WARNING: Low temperatures and excessive watering in winter. will prove fatal.

• Plant Identification p.23   • Propagation by Cuttings p.181   • Pests pp.194–196   • Checklists pp.212–217

PEACE LILY

Spathiphyllum wallisii
Height: 23—30 cm
Spread: 25—38 cm

The bright green, lance-shaped leaves of this evergreen are 7.5 cm wide, 15 cm long and are borne on stiff, upright, 15-cm stalks. They splay outward.

From May to August, the peace lily bears pure white, arum-like flowers on 20-cm stems, which rise well above the leaves.

S. × 'Mauna Loa' grows to 45—50 cm high, has larger flowers and leaves, but is less hardy than *S. wallisii*. From May to October, and intermittently throughout the year if it is kept warm and humid, it bears large, white flowers rising on 45-cm stalks above the leaves.

SURVIVAL BASICS

Light and temperature: Bright sunlight in winter, but diffused light in summer; winter temperature of 10°C (50°F). *S.* × 'Mauna Loa' needs a winter minimum of 13°C (55°F).

Watering and feeding: Keep compost moist in winter; water freely in summer. From April to September, add a weak liquid fertilizer every 3 weeks.

Compost and repotting: Use John Innes potting compost No. 2, or a peat-based type. Repot in spring, if potbound.

Propagation: By division in spring.

WARNING: Low temperatures and waterlogged compost are fatal.

COLOMBIA

Yellow, dried-out leaves are due to strong sunlight. Move to a shadier spot.

Shrivelled leaves indicate a dry compost. Stand the plant in a bucket of water for a couple of hours, then allow the excess water to drain away.

PESTS AND DISEASES
Red spider mites
Mealy bugs
Greenfly

• Plant Identification p.9   • Propagation by Division p.179   • Pests pp.194—196   • Checklists pp.212—217

TI LOG PLANT

Cordyline terminalis
Height: 45–90 cm
Spread: 38–45 cm

This striking evergreen, also known as *C. fruticosa*, has a central stem clothed with long-stemmed, narrow leaves when young. With age, some of the lower leaves fall off and the plant resembles a palm. The lance-shaped leaves are light crimson when they first appear, then slowly become bronze-green, with pinkish-red shading at the edges. They can grow to 10 cm wide and 60 cm long.

Colourful forms include 'Tricolor' (dark green leaves variegated with pink, red and cream); 'Firebrand' (curving reddish leaves); 'Guilfoylei' (pink, red and white striped leaves); and 'Rededge' (bright reddish-purple leaves with green markings).

Ti, part of the common name, is used for any of several cordyline shrubs and trees from tropical Asia and nearby Pacific regions. The full common name reflects the recent popularity of imported log-like cuttings that can be potted up.

The cabbage tree, *C. australis*, grows as a small tree in its native Australia and New Zealand. As a houseplant, it will only reach 60–90 cm in height and 45–60 cm in width. The strap-like, dull green leaves eventually fall in an arching, fountain-like cluster from the top of the central stem. Indoors it seldom flowers, but in mild climates, where it can be placed outdoors in summer, it occasionally produces white blooms.

The grass palm, *C. indivisa*, grows as a small palm-like tree in its native New Zealand, but in a pot will only reach 0.9–1.2 m high. A single stem produces a wealth of narrow, arching, medium green leaves with yellow or red midribs.

CORDYLINE TERMINALIS
'TRICOLOR'
The green leaves are 30 cm long and splashed with red, pink and cream.

CORDYLINE TERMINALIS
'REDEDGE'
The dark green leaves are 22 cm long with red streaks and a red margin.

SURVIVAL BASICS

Light and temperature: Bright, indirect sunlight; winter temperatures of 10–13°C (50–55°F).

Watering and feeding: Keep compost just moist in winter; water freely in summer. From April to September, add a weak liquid fertilizer every 2 weeks.

Compost and repotting: Use John Innes potting compost No. 2 or a peat-based type. Repot in spring, when potbound, usually every 2 years.

Propagation: Take 7.5-cm stem cuttings from old leggy plants.

WARNING: Low temperatures and waterlogged compost are fatal.

• Plant Identification p.23

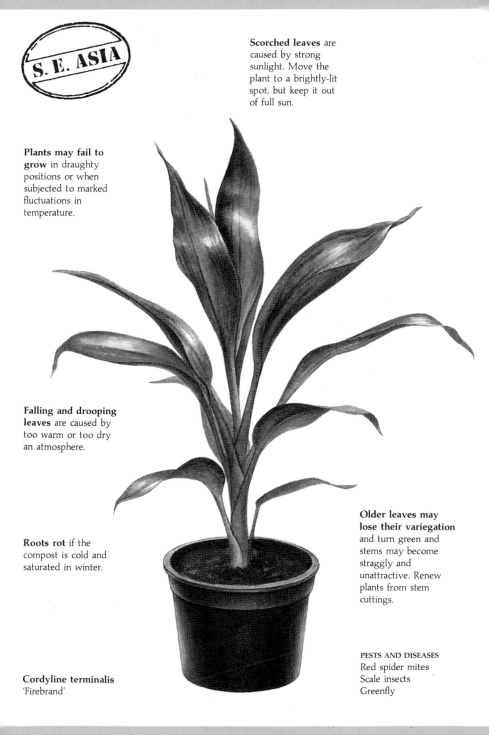

S. E. ASIA

Scorched leaves are caused by strong sunlight. Move the plant to a brightly-lit spot, but keep it out of full sun.

Plants may fail to grow in draughty positions or when subjected to marked fluctuations in temperature.

Falling and drooping leaves are caused by too warm or too dry an atmosphere.

Roots rot if the compost is cold and saturated in winter.

Older leaves may lose their variegation and turn green and stems may become straggly and unattractive. Renew plants from stem cuttings.

Cordyline terminalis 'Firebrand'

PESTS AND DISEASES
Red spider mites
Scale insects
Greenfly

• Propagation by Cuttings p.181

• Pests pp.194–196
• Checklists pp.212–217

DEVIL'S IVY

Epipremnum pinnatum 'Aureum'
Height: 1.2–1.5 m – climbs or trails
Spread: 38–45 cm

This familiar houseplant, widely sold as *Scindapsus aureus*, can either trail or be trained to climb a moss-covered pole.

The juvenile leaves are glossy, oval, slightly pointed and dark green. As the plant matures, they become elongated, more pointed, heart-shaped, bright green and splashed with yellow.

Two other forms that are rather more difficult to grow are 'Marble Queen' (leaves marbled and thickly covered in white) and 'Golden Queen' (leaves almost completely dappled yellow).

A related species, *Scindapsus pictus*, has heart-shaped, bluish-green leaves with silver spots and a thin white line along the edges.

Rotting stems and limp leaves are caused by low winter temperatures and draughts, combined with overwatering.

Shrivelled, brown leaf tips are caused by a dry atmosphere. Mist the plant regularly.

Leaf variegations are lost because of inadequate lighting.

PESTS AND DISEASES
Red spider mites

SURVIVAL BASICS

Light and temperature: Bright, indirect sunlight; winter temperatures of 13–15°C (55–59°F).

Watering and feeding: Keep compost just damp in winter. Water freely in summer, but let the compost dry out between waterings. From May to September, add a weak liquid fertilizer every 4 weeks.

Compost and repotting: Use an acid, peat-based compost. Repot in spring, usually every 2–3 years.

Propagation: Divide and repot congested plants in spring, or take stem cuttings in spring or early summer.

WARNING: Cold, waterlogged compost will rot the roots.

• Plant Identification p.14   • Propagation by Cuttings pp.176–178   • Propagation by Division p.179   • Pests pp.194–196   • Checklists pp.212–217

If the leaves become discoloured, it is probably because the compost is waterlogged. Remove the plant from the pot to allow the compost to dry out. If the compost is too dry, soak the rootball in water for an hour or two.

Yellow, wilting leaves result if temperatures are too low. Leaves also wilt if the compost is too wet or too dry.

PESTS AND
DISEASES
Mealy bugs

SWEETHEART PLANT

Philodendron scandens
Height: 1–1.5 m – climbs or trails
Spread: 20–38 cm

The sweetheart plant is so easy to grow that it is extremely popular. The medium to dark green, glossy, 10 cm-long, heart-shaped leaves turn deep green with age.

The elephant's ear, *P. domesticum*, often sold as *P. hastatum*, has spear-shaped, medium green leaves, up to 18 cm long.

The blushing philodendron, *P. erubescens*, is a vigorous climber. Its arrow-shaped, glossy, dark green leaves have a coppery tinge. The most attractive form is 'Burgundy', with bright coppery-red leaves that turn olive-green with age.

Black gold, *P. melanochrysum*, has heart-shaped leaves which, when mature, are dark green with ivory veins and a coppery sheen, and up to 60 cm long.

SURVIVAL BASICS

Light and temperature: Bright, indirect sunlight; winter temperatures of 13–18°C (55–64°F).
Watering and feeding: Keep compost just moist in winter; water freely in summer. From May to September, add a weak liquid fertilizer every 2 weeks.
Compost and repotting: Use peat-based compost plus some coarse sand. Repot in spring, when roots are congested, usually every other year.
Propagation: Take stem-tip cuttings in spring.

WARNING: Mist aerial roots regularly, especially in summer, to prevent them from hardening.

• Plant Identification p.18   • Propagation by Cuttings pp.176–178   • Pests pp.194–196   • Checklists pp.212–217

PELARGONIUM

Pelargonium × hortorum
Height: 30–60 cm, some larger
Spread: 25–45 cm

The various types of pelargonium, often referred to as geraniums, are prized for their summer flowers and their distinctive leaves. They are often confused with the hardy herbaceous plants belonging to the genus *Geranium*.

The zonal pelargoniums, derived from *P. zonale*, have rounded leaves, 7.5–10 cm wide. They are light to medium green, with maroon or bronze 'horseshoe' zones of colour. The flowers are 12–25 mm wide and are available in colours including pink, red, salmon, purple and white. There are a number of different forms: single, double, cactus-shaped with five narrow petals, and star-shaped with wider petals.

The regal pelargoniums, derived from *P. domesticum*, are 38–60 cm high, erect and branching with scalloped-edged, rounded, medium green leaves. The flowers are 4–5 cm wide, frilly-edged and available in shades of pink, salmon, red, purple and white. They are marked or veined with a darker shade of the same colour. Flowers and leaves are borne on thin, brittle stems, unlike those of zonal pelargoniums which are thick and brittle.

The ivy-leaved pelargoniums, derived from *P. peltatum*, are also known as trailing pelargoniums. The stems trail for up to 90 cm, and bear deeply-lobed, fleshy, medium green leaves that resemble those of ivy. The pink, red or white, star-shaped flowers come in single or double forms.

The lemon-scented geranium, *P. crispum*, grows 45–60 cm high and has crisp, wedge-shaped, three-lobed leaves which, as their common name suggests, have a strong lemon fragrance.

PELARGONIUM DOMESTICUM
Varieties have few, large blooms contrastingly marked in distinctive colours.

PELARGONIUM PELTATUM
Varieties have single or double blooms in one or a mixture of colours.
Variety illustrated:
'Rouletti'

PELARGONIUM CRISPUM
Leaves densely arranged, medium green and wedge-shaped.
Variety illustrated:
'Variegatum'

SURVIVAL BASICS

Light and temperature: Bright sunlight; winter temperatures of 7–10°C (45–50°F).

Watering and feeding: Keep compost barely moist in winter; water freely in summer, especially when in flower. Add a weak liquid fertilizer every 10–14 days from May to September.

Compost and repotting: Use John Innes potting compost No. 2. Repot every spring.

Propagation: Take stem cuttings in summer.

WARNING: Keep in good light, otherwise the plants become spindly and their lower leaves fall off.

• Plant Identification
p.13, p.20

Leaf edges turn red if the temperature falls below the recommended winter minimum.

Yellowing foliage and dead leaves and flowers, besides being unsightly, make the plant susceptible to disease. Check and remove them regularly.

High winter temperatures discourage flowering in regal pelargoniums.

Leaves turn yellow due to under- or overwatering. Check the compost regularly and remedy as appropriate.

Pelargonium zonale

PESTS AND DISEASES
Grey mould
Black leg
Whitefly
Greenfly
Vine weevils

HYBRID

• Propagation by Cuttings pp.176–178   • Pests pp.194–196   • Diseases p.197
• Checklists pp.212–217

PARASOL PLANT

Schefflera arboricola
Height: 1.5–1.8 m
Spread: 45–75 cm

This tree-like evergreen, also called *Heptapleurum arboricola*, grows rapidly to its full height. Each branch is about 25 cm long and ends in a parasol-shaped array of seven or more arching, glossy, green leaflets.

The parasol plant can be kept low and bushy by nipping out the growing tip when it is young, although some people consider a taller plant more elegant.

The slow-growing but larger umbrella tree or umbrella plant, *Brassaia actinophylla*, which is better known as *Schefflera actinophylla*, reaches 1.8–2.4 m high and 60–90 cm wide. Its long side stems bear four or five leaflets. With age, these increase to 12 or more in number.

SURVIVAL BASICS

Light and temperature: Bright, indirect sunlight; winter temperature of 13°C (55°F).

Watering and feeding: Keep compost barely moist in winter; water freely in summer. From April to September, add a weak liquid fertilizer every 2–3 weeks.

Compost and repotting: Use John Innes potting compost No. 2. Repot in spring, when potbound, every 2–3 years.

Propagation: Take stem cuttings 7.5 cm-long in spring, or sow seeds.

WARNING: Sudden changes in temperature or watering cause leaves to fall.

Plants will grow used to light shade, even though they are best grown in indirect sunlight. Do not move them suddenly from good to poor light.

A large plant often loses its lower leaves, no matter how well it is cared for. In a group of other floor-standing plants, foliage from low-growing species will conceal its naked base.

Wilting leaves result from too much or too little moisture. Leaves with blackened tips indicate too much water, while yellowing is due to too little water. Remember to check the compost before watering.

PESTS AND DISEASES
Greenfly

• Plant Identification p.31   • Propagation by Cuttings pp.176–178   • Pests pp.194–196   • Checklists pp.212–217

SWISS CHEESE PLANT

Monstera deliciosa
Height: 3.5–4.5 m
Spread: 1.5–2.1 m

The large, holed and deeply lobed, shiny, deep green leaves of this vigorous climber make it a unique houseplant. The leathery adult leaves may eventually reach 75 cm or more long and 45 cm wide.

Its aerial roots are not only a means of anchoring the plant to a pole or support; they can also absorb water and minerals. A moss-covered pole will provide support for your plant — keep the pole constantly moist and train the roots around it.

M. deliciosa can grow too large for the home. The smaller form, *M. d. borsigiana*, a plant with equally attractive leaf perforations, is an excellent alternative.

SURVIVAL BASICS

Light and temperature: Bright, indirect sunlight; winter temperature of 10°C (50°F).

Watering and feeding: Keep compost damp in winter. Water freely in summer but allow compost to dry out between waterings. From April to September, add a weak liquid fertilizer every 3–4 weeks.

Compost and repotting: Use John Innes potting compost No. 3, or a peat-based mix. Repot in spring.

Propagation: Take stem-tip cuttings from tall plants in early summer.

WARNING: Cold or waterlogged compost will prove fatal.

MEXICO

Pale leaves and spindly growth result from too much shade. Move the plant to better light, but not strong sunlight.

Yellow leaves that do not wilt are due to insufficient feeding.

Yellow wilting leaves result from a saturated compost. Withhold water until the compost dries out.

Keep the compost fairly dry if the temperature falls below 10°C (50°F).

Brown leaf edges are caused by low temperatures.

Papery and brown leaf edges are caused by a dry atmosphere.

PESTS AND DISEASES
Red spider mites
Mealy bugs

• Plant Identification p.21   • Propagation by Cuttings pp.176–178   • Pests pp.194–196   • Checklists pp.212–217

ZEBRA PLANT

Aphelandra squarrosa
Height: 25–60 cm
Spread: 30–38 cm

Both the flowers and the foliage make this tropical shrub one of the most colourful of all houseplants. The large, spear-shaped, glossy, dark green leaves have striking ivory veins. They are 23 cm long and are arranged in pairs on opposite sides of a stout, central stem.

From July to September, the leaves are crowned with striking cone-shaped flower heads. These are, in fact, closely overlapping, bright yellow bracts, 7.5–10 cm long. Each of these flower heads lasts for six to eight weeks. The true flowers, which are small, tubular and yellow, emerge from these heads but wither after a few days. Remove the flower heads as soon as they begin to fade by cutting them off cleanly with a sharp knife.

Attractive varieties include 'Louisae', a sturdy plant that grows up to 75 cm high. Its leaves are narrower and veined in white, and its yellow flower heads are streaked with red. 'Dania' is similar but shorter and more compact, at 30 cm high and 20–23 cm wide.

Two other aphelandras are sometimes grown as houseplants. The fiery spike, *A. aurantiaca*, has elliptical, light green leaves that are 10–23 cm long and have greyish veins. The brilliant orange-yellow flower heads are tinged with scarlet.

The pagoda plant, *A. chamissoniana*, has slender, pointed, close-set, green leaves that are 10–13 cm long and have silvery-white veins. The flower head is 4 cm long and tapers to a point. The bright yellow bracts are tipped with green and the true flowers are clear yellow.

APHELANDRA CHAMISSONIANA
Overlapping, bright yellow bracts taper to a point.

APHELANDRA AURANTIACA
The orange-yellow flower bracts are tinged with scarlet.

SURVIVAL BASICS

Light and temperature: Bright, indirect sunlight; winter temperature of 10°C (50°F).

Watering and feeding: Keep compost moist in winter, but never let it dry out. Water freely in summer. From April to September, add a weak liquid fertilizer every week. Feed every 2 weeks at other times.

Compost and repotting: Use John Innes potting compost No. 2. Repot in spring, when potbound.

Propagation: Take stem-tip cuttings 7.5–10 cm long in spring.

WARNING: Never let the temperature fall below the recommended winter minimum.

• Plant Identification p.27

New growth in spring is especially susceptible to attack by aphids and scale insects. Regularly check the growing points and take steps to prevent these pests from establishing themselves and spreading.

Leggy plants with few leaves need regular feeding.

To encourage shoots suitable for cuttings, cut back the plant after flowering. Leave a pair of healthy leaves on each shoot. In spring, detach and root the new shoots.

BRAZIL

Poor growth results unless compost is kept moist throughout the year.

Aphelandra squarrosa

PESTS AND DISEASES
Greenfly
Scale insects

• Propagation by Cuttings pp.176–178
• Pests pp.194–196
• Checklists pp.212–217

RUBBER PLANT

Ficus elastica
Height: 0.9–1.2 m
Spread: 38–45 cm

This common houseplant, if grown in a large enough tub, can easily reach a height of 3.5 m. Most indoor specimens will be much smaller because their roots are restricted to a pot of standard size. Plants usually form a single stem with large, shiny, dark green leaves up to 30 cm long.

The many variegated forms are very popular. They include 'Tricolor' (green leaves variegated in cream and flushed pink); 'Variegata' (silvery-grey and white markings); and 'Schryveriana' (green leaves with cream patches). The minimum winter temperature for *F. elastica* and its varieties is 16°C (61°F).

The creeping fig, *F. pumila*, has dark green, heart-shaped leaves, and will creep, trail or climb. In a small pot, it climbs or trails 45–60 cm. It needs a minimum winter temperature of 10°C (50°F).

The weeping fig, *F. benjamina*, forms a magnificent weeping shrub, 1.2–1.8 m high. Its graceful arching branches bear slender-pointed leaves; soft green at first, they darken later. It needs a minimum winter temperature of 13°C (55°F).

The mistletoe fig, *F. deltoidea*, is compact and bushy; it grows to 45–75 cm high and 38–45 cm wide. The small, oval leaves are dark green. Its common name comes from the clusters of yellow-grey berries borne from the leaf joints throughout the year. It needs a minimum winter temperature of 10°C (50°F).

The fiddleback fig, *F. lyrata*, grows 1.2–1.5 m high, with fiddle-shaped, glossy, dark green leaves. They are up to 38 cm long, wavy-edged and veined in a pale, yellowish-green. It needs a minimum winter temperature of 13°C (55°F).

FICUS PUMILA
'VARIEGATA'
The delicate, dark green leaves have tiny white or cream spots.

FICUS BENJAMINA
The small, apple-green leaves darken with age.

FICUS LYRATA
Large, gleaming, medium green leaves have wavy edges.

SURVIVAL BASICS

Light and temperature: Bright, indirect sunlight; winter temperatures of 10–16°C (50–61°F), according to species.

Watering and feeding: Keep compost just moist in winter; water freely in summer. From May to September, add a weak liquid fertilizer every 10–14 days.

Compost and repotting: Use John Innes potting compost No. 2, or peat-based types. Repot in spring.

Propagation: Air-layer large, bare-stemmed plants.

WARNING: Young leaves are easily damaged, causing scars that remain for the rest of the plant's life.

• Plant Identification
pp.30–31

Sponge shiny leaves gently and regularly with clean water to remove accumulated dirt and dust. Do not do this in strong sunlight.

Yellowing leaves can be due to insufficient feeding or old age.

TROPICAL ASIA

Saturated compost, especially in winter, causes the leaves of rubber plants to fall off. Cold conditions and draughts have the same effect on other large ficus plants. The weeping fig is especially vulnerable in cold draughts.

Ficus elastica 'Decora'

PESTS AND DISEASES
Red spider mites
Scale insects
Mealy bugs

• Propagation by Air-layering p.180
• Pests pp.194–196
• Checklists pp.212–217

ROSE OF CHINA

Hibiscus rosa-sinensis
Height: 45–60 cm
Spread: 38–45 cm

This exotic shrub can grow 1.5–1.8 m high in a large tub outdoors or in a conservatory. Indoors, its growth should be restrained by cutting back the shoots to within 15 cm of their base in early spring.

The coarsely-toothed, oval, pointed, dark green leaves are 2.5 cm wide and 5–7.5 cm long. The deep crimson flowers that appear from June to September are funnel-shaped, about 13 cm wide, and papery in texture. Each flower has a central spire of golden stamens 5 cm long. Though the blooms last only a day or two, they are produced over a long period.

Several varieties are available, with double or semi-double flowers, and in yellow, pink, salmon or white.

The variegated rose of China, *H. rosa-sinensis* 'Cooperi', is smaller and more compact, with crimson flowers and cream and crimson variegated leaves.

Two other evergreen, but tender, hibiscus shrubs can be grown indoors, though they do better in greenhouses or conservatories. *H. mutabilis* can grow to 1.8 m, and has medium green, heart-shaped, downy leaves. However, when grown in a pot 15–20 cm wide, it can be restrained, with spring pruning, to 90 cm high. The flowers often last for only a day. They are 10 cm wide, initially pale pink or white, then changing to deep red as the day progresses.

H. moscheutos grows up to 2.4 m high outdoors but will not reach this indoors, even in a greenhouse border. Usually grown in the hybrid form, 'Southern Belle', its height and spread are 1.2–1.5 m. The large flowers, in white, pink, rose or crimson, first appear in the second year.

SINGLE
Hibiscus rosa-sinensis hybrid

FRILLY-EDGED SINGLE
Hibiscus rosa-sinensis hybrid

SEMI-DOUBLE
Hibiscus rosa-sinensis hybrid

SURVIVAL BASICS

Light and temperature: Bright, indirect sunlight; winter temperatures of 13–15°C (55–59°F).

Watering and feeding: Keep compost barely moist in winter; water freely in summer. From May to September, add a weak liquid fertilizer every 2–3 weeks.

Compost and repotting: Use John Innes potting compost No. 2, or a peat-based type. Repot each spring, when pruning.

Propagation: Take 10-cm stem or stem-tip cuttings in summer.

WARNING: Keep the compost moist or the leaves will drop.

• Plant Identification p.10

CHINA

Yellowing or falling leaves result from incorrect watering or feeding.

Prune the plant severely in spring when new growth resumes. Cut back stems and branches to a height of about 15 cm and give more water.

Flower buds and lower leaves will soon drop if the compost becomes dry. Draughts also cause the buds and leaves to fall.

Hibiscus plants need as much light as possible throughout the year. Ideally, they should have some sunshine every day — but avoid strong, summer sun.

Leaves curl at their edges if the atmosphere is dry. Mist the plant frequently.

Hibiscus rosa-sinensis

PESTS AND DISEASES
Red spider mites
Greenfly

• Propagation by Cuttings pp.176–178
• Pests pp.194–196
• Checklists pp.212–217

PIGGY-BACK PLANT

Tolmiea menziesii
Height: 15 cm
Spread: 38 cm

The piggy-back plant can tolerate a range of temperatures, reaching as low as 4°C (39°F). Its central stem is almost hidden by the heart-shaped leaves which are characterized, when mature, by the plantlets growing from them. The hairy, maple-like, medium green leaves are 5 cm wide and borne on leaf stalks up to 10 cm long. The plantlets grow from the top surface of the leaves, at the junction with the leaf stalks. Their weight bends the leaf stalks so they appear to trail.

Occasionally in summer, the piggy-back plant produces insignificant, red-flushed, greenish-white, tubular flowers on stems up to 60 cm long.

In **summer**, mist the leaves regularly to deter red spider mites.

SURVIVAL BASICS

Light and temperature: Bright, but lightly shaded. Will also grow for short periods in deeper shade. Winter temperatures of 4–7°C (39–45°F).

Watering and feeding: Keep compost barely moist in winter, but water freely in summer. From May to September, apply a weak liquid fertilizer every 2–3 weeks.

Compost and repotting: Use John Innes potting compost No. 2. Repot in spring, when potbound.

Propagation: Pot up a mature leaf, with 2.5 cm stalk and plantlet.

WARNING: Hot, dry air will kill the plant.

Winter temperatures below those recommended cause leaves to die and fall off. If low temperatures are unavoidable in winter, keep the compost only barely moist. A combination of a low temperature and saturated compost will certainly kill the plant.

Yellow mottling is due to red spider mites, probably encouraged by a dry atmosphere.

PESTS AND DISEASES
Red spider mites
Greenfly

• Plant Identification p.30   • Propagation by Plantlets p.181   • Pests pp.194–196   • Checklists pp.212–217

Dry, brown leaf edges can be caused by a dry atmosphere or an attack of red spider mites. Mist the foliage regularly.

Variegated leaves may revert to all-green if kept in too much shade.

PESTS AND
DISEASES
Red spider mites
Scale insects

COMMON IVY

Hedera helix
Height: 45—90 cm
Spread: climbing or trailing

This hardy, scrambling climber is the parent of many small-leaved, moderately vigorous houseplants. Most are ideal for cool, shaded situations that other plants will not tolerate.

The leaves of these ivies vary widely in the number, shape and size of their lobes. The most attractive varieties include the goldenheart ivy, *Hedera helix* 'Jubilee' (three-lobed, tapering, dark green leaves with yellow centres); *H. h.* 'Glacier' (three-lobed, variegated silver-grey with creamy-white edges); the needlepoint ivy, *H. h.* 'Sagittaefolia' (five-lobed, all-green leaves, the central lobe long and pointed).

SURVIVAL BASICS

Light and temperature: Bright sunlight, indirect light in summer; winter temperatures of 4—7°C (39—45°F).
Watering and feeding: Water sparingly in winter, but freely in summer. Apply a weak liquid fertilizer every 2—3 weeks in summer.
Compost and repotting: Use John Innes potting compost No. 2. Repot in spring, when congested, usually every other year.
Propagation: Take 7.5—10 cm-long stem cuttings in summer.

WARNING: Keep winter temperatures below 15°C (59°F), especially when the light is poor.

• Plant Identification p.19   • Propagation by Cuttings   • Pests pp.194—196
                                  pp.176—178   • Checklists pp.212—217

FAIRY PRIMROSE

Primula malacoides
Height: 30–38 cm
Spread: 30–45 cm

This attractive perennial is usually grown as an annual, which means that fresh plants are raised each year. The pale green leaves are hairy, oval and tooth-edged. Fragrant flowers are 12 mm wide and grow in tiered whorls from December to April. They range in colour from pale purple to red and white. Each flower has a central yellow 'eye'.

The poison primrose, *P. obconica*, is another perennial. The oval to heart-shaped, light green leaves are covered in hairs that are poisonous and cause skin rashes in some people, especially on the insides of the wrist. The allergic reaction is likely to be more severe when the leaves are damp.

The pink, red, lilac or blue flowers of the poison primrose are 2.5 cm wide and borne in clusters on stems 30 cm long from December to May. Each flower has a green 'eye'. Many larger-flowered varieties are available in a rich assortment of colours.

The Chinese primrose, *P. praenitens*, better known as *P. sinensis*, has rosettes of medium green leaves that are hairy, lobed, toothed, and broadly oval in shape. From December to March, the plant produces 30 cm-long stems with whorls of flowers, 2.5–4 cm across and usually frilly-edged, in colours including white, pink, red, orange or purple. Each flower has a central yellow 'eye'.

P. × kewensis has spoon-shaped, tooth-edged leaves covered with a white, waxy powder. From midwinter to spring, it bears 2 cm-wide, fragrant, yellow flowers in tiered whorls on upright stems that are 25 cm long.

PRIMULA MALACOIDES
Small fragrant flowers in white, purple, lilac, pink or various shades of red.

PRIMULA OBCONICA
Large fragrant flowers in blue, lilac, pink or red have a green 'eye'.

PRIMULA PRAENITENS
Attractive, frilly-edged, red flowers offset by bright yellow, star-shaped centres.

SURVIVAL BASICS

Light and temperature: Bright, indirect sunlight; winter temperatures of 13–15°C (55–59°F).

Watering and feeding: Keep compost moist, especially during flowering. Feed every 2 weeks with a weak liquid fertilizer once the flower buds are formed.

Compost and repotting: Use John Innes potting compost No. 1 or 2.

Propagation: Sow seeds from May to July.

WARNING: High temperatures will kill primulas, especially if the compost is dry.

• Plant Identification p.9

CHINA

Continued blooming can be encouraged by removing faded and dead flowers. Pull them off with the stalks still attached.

Yellowing of young leaves may be due to lack of magnesium. Rectify this with a dilute solution of Epsom salts.

Yellow foliage may result if the plant is kept in a hot, dry place. It may also be caused by the alkalinity of hard tapwater.

Brown leaf edges and brown patches on leaves are caused by excessively low temperatures in winter.

Mottled foliage is caused by a dry compost. Keep the compost moist at all times.

PESTS AND DISEASES
Greenfly
Caterpillars
Grey mould

Primula × kewensis

• Pests pp.194–196   • Diseases p.197
• Checklists pp.212–217

ARROWHEAD VINE

Syngonium podophyllum
Height: 0.9–1.8 m
Spread: 38–45 cm

This vine forms a bushy plant at first, but with age, it climbs or trails. When young, the shiny, medium to dark green leaves are arrow-shaped and borne on erect stems. As the leaves mature, they develop irregular ear-like lobes at the base, producing an unusual shape. With age, the lobes divide, eventually forming as many as nine separate leaflets. The appearance of lobed leaves indicates that the plant is about to climb.

In addition to 'Emerald Gem', a common form that has shiny, dark green leaves with silvery-white markings, there are varieties with variegated foliage, such as 'Green Gold' and 'Emerald Green'.

SURVIVAL BASICS

Light and temperature: Bright, but indirect light for variegated types; light shade for all-green forms; winter temperature of 15°C (59°F).
Watering and feeding: Keep compost moist, especially in summer, but avoid waterlogging. From April to September, add a weak liquid fertilizer every 2–3 weeks.
Compost and repotting: Use John Innes potting compost No. 2, with additional peat. Repot in spring, every other year.
Propagation: Take stem-tip cuttings in late spring or summer.

WARNING: Do not let aerial roots of climbing forms become dry.

Variegated leaves lose their attractive colourings and revert to all green if plants are kept in dark positions.

Keep the vine bushy by cutting off the climbing stems as they form. Cut each stem back to just above a leaf joint.

Roots soon rot if the recommended winter temperature cannot be maintained and the compost is too wet. If the temperature falls, water less frequently.

PESTS AND DISEASES
Greenfly
Red spider mites

PINK JASMINE

Jasminum polyanthum
Height: 0.9–1.5 m
Spread: 0.9–1.2 m

This climber is easy to train up a permanent trellis in a conservatory or around a group of pliable canes indoors where it flowers from November to April. The blooms are highly fragrant, star-shaped and pale pink or white. They are 2.5 cm across and borne in clusters, up to 13 cm long, among dark green leaves composed of five to seven leaflets. A jasmine plant will flower in its first year, unlike many climbing and flowering houseplants.
Also recommended:
J. mesnyi, the primrose jasmine: Produces scentless, semi-double, yellow flowers from March to May.

SURVIVAL BASICS

Light and temperature: Bright light, but protect from strong summer sunlight; winter temperatures of 7–10°C (45–50°F).
Watering and feeding: Keep compost moist, and feed every 2 weeks with a weak liquid fertilizer when the plant is in flower.
Compost and repotting: Use John Innes potting compost No. 2. Repot in spring, when potbound.
Propagation: From 7.5–10 cm stem or stem-tip cuttings in August or September.

WARNING: Do not exceed the recommended winter temperatures.

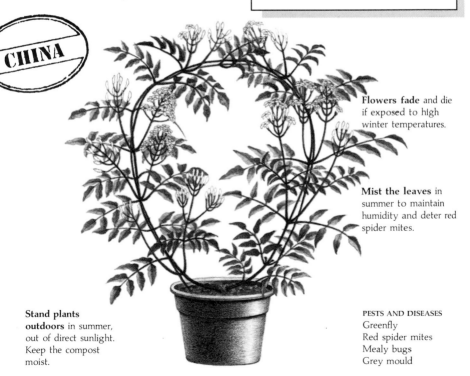

CHINA

Flowers fade and die if exposed to high winter temperatures.

Mist the leaves in summer to maintain humidity and deter red spider mites.

Stand plants outdoors in summer, out of direct sunlight. Keep the compost moist.

PESTS AND DISEASES
Greenfly
Red spider mites
Mealy bugs
Grey mould

• Plant Identification p.13   • Propagation by Cuttings pp.176–178   • Pests pp.194–196   • Diseases p.197   • Checklists pp.212–217

SLIPPER PLANT

Calceolaria × herbeohybrida
Height: 20–45 cm
Spread: 20–38 cm

CALCEOLARIA ×
HERBEOHYBRIDA
'MULTIFLORA NANA'
Masses of small
flowers in red, orange
or yellow.

The spectacular flowers of this bushy plant are an unusual, pouch-like shape. They are 2.5–5 cm wide and are available in shades of yellow, orange, red, pink or brown. Most varieties are spotted or splashed with crimson.

The large, oval to heart-shaped leaves grow up to 20 cm across and are hairy, soft and medium green in colour. Several tall stalks (from 30–60 cm) rise above them, each bearing clusters of flowers.

CALCEOLARIA ×
HERBEOHYBRIDA
'GRANDIFLORA'
Large yellow or red
flowers have maroon
or brown-red spots.

The flowering time is from May to July. Buy a plant when the pouched flowers are just opening, with more buds still to open; it should remain in flower for four to five weeks.

There are several varieties available in a wide range of heights and colours. The 'Multiflora Nana' hybrids are compact plants about 23 cm high, with masses of small flowers. 'Glorious Formula Mixed' hybrids are 30 cm high, with large pouched heads.

'Intermediate Special Hybrids' are taller, at 38 cm, with medium-sized pouches. Even taller, at 45 cm, is 'Perfection Mixed', with huge pouches, some single-coloured and others brightly striped.

Calceolaria integrifolia is widely grown outdoors in summer, but it can also be grown in pots indoors. The variety frequently grown indoors is 'Sunshine', which is 20–25 cm high. From July to September, the bushy, compact plant produces a wealth of small, pouched, rich yellow flowers. The clusters of blooms rise well above the matt, finely wrinkled, oblong to lance-shaped, medium green leaves.

SURVIVAL BASICS

Light and temperature: Bright indirect sunlight; winter temperatures of 10–15°C (50–59°F).

Watering and feeding: Keep compost moist and feed with a weak liquid fertilizer every 10 days, especially when in flower.

Compost and repotting: Use John Innes potting compost No. 1 or 2, or a peat-based type. Unless raising plants from seed, repotting is unnecessary. Discard after flowering.

Propagation: Sow seeds in late spring at 18–21°C (64–70°F).

WARNING: Dry compost, high temperatures and draughts can cause the plant to collapse.

• Plant Identification p.9

HYBRID

Wilting plants result either from dry or saturated compost. If dry, stand the pot in a bucket of water for an hour or so. If too wet, withhold water until the compost dries.

Yellowing foliage is usually due to lack of nutrients. Feed the plant every 10 days.

Always water from below. Water droplets on the soft, hairy leaves will concentrate the sun's rays and cause burn marks.

Prolong the plant's life by increasing the humidity. Stand it in a tray of moist pebbles.

PESTS AND DISEASES
Greenfly
Leafhoppers
Whitefly

Calceolaria
× herbeohybrida

• Pests pp.194–196
• Checklists pp.212–217

IRON CROSS BEGONIA

Begonia masoniana
Height: 20–25 cm
Spread: 25–30 cm

Several species of begonia are grown predominantly for their attractive foliage. *B. masoniana* has puckered, obliquely heart-shaped, medium green leaves that are covered in red hairs. Each leaf is 15 cm long, 15 cm wide and has an eye-catching central 'cross' composed of four or five bronze-purple arms.

The rex begonia, *Begonia rex*, also has obliquely heart-shaped leaves. They grow up to 25 cm long, have wrinkled surfaces and are dark green with silvery bands close to the edges. Its many varieties are more popular than the true species and include 'Merry Christmas' (maroon-red leaves with green, silver and pink bands) and 'King Edward IV' (purple-red leaves with pink spots).

The eyelash begonia, *Begonia boweri*, is a bushy plant, growing 15–25 cm tall. Its obliquely heart-shaped, emerald-green leaves are 7.5 cm long. Their edges and stalks are both chocolate-brown and covered with erect hairs. In late winter and early spring, the plant bears tiny white or pale pink flowers.

The metallic leaf begonia, *Begonia metallica*, has branching stems bearing obliquely heart-shaped leaves 15 cm long. Their metallic-green surface is covered with white hairs and lined with purple veins. In late summer, the plant bears small whitish flowers.

The lettuce-leaf begonia, *Begonia × feastii* 'Bunchii', has medium green leaves with unusual, frilled and crested edges and red undersides edged with long white hairs. From midwinter to late spring, the plant produces clusters of pale pink flowers 12 mm across.

BEGONIA REX
Many varieties with large leaves in a wide range of colours, often marked with spots or blotches.

BEGONIA BOWERI
Leaf edges chocolate-brown with erect hairs.

SURVIVAL BASICS

Light and temperature: Bright, indirect sunlight; winter temperature of 13 °C (55 °F).

Watering and feeding: Water sparingly in winter. At other times keep compost moist but not continually saturated. Feed with a weak liquid fertilizer every 10–14 days from spring to autumn.

Compost and repotting: Use John Innes potting compost No. 1. Repot in spring, when potbound.

Propagation: Take leaf cuttings, or divide the plant, in May or June.

WARNING: Begonias will become untidy and lose their leaf colours if left for too long in the same compost.

• Plant Identification p.27

S. E. ASIA

Small 'burn' holes will appear on the leaves if water is splashed on them while the plant is standing in strong sunlight.

Begonias collapse if the air is too dry. Stand the pot in a tray of wet pebbles or surround it with moist peat. Keep the atmosphere humid, but never wet the leaves.

Plants become lop-sided if they are left for too long standing in the same position. Encourage balanced growth all round by turning the pot periodically.

Roots soon rot if the compost is kept saturated, especially in winter. Always allow the surface to dry out before watering.

Begonia masoniana

PESTS AND DISEASES
Tarsonemid mites
Botrytis

• Propagation by Cuttings pp.176–178

• Propagation by Division p.179

• Diseases p.197
• Pests pp.194–196

• Checklists pp.212–217

BEGONIA

Begonia × tuberhybrida
Height: 30–50 cm
Spread: 30–38 cm

Among the most popular flowering begonias, this plant grows, as its scientific name suggests, from a tuber that lies just below the surface of the compost. It bears many single or double flowers, 7.5–13 cm across, amid oval to heart-shaped leaves that are dark green, slightly lobed, serrated and 15–20 cm long.

The large, rose-like flowers bloom from June to September. They are arranged in groups of three and are available in a wide range of colours. Named varieties include 'Olympia' (bright crimson), 'Seville' (yellow, with a bright pink edge) and 'Festiva' (bright yellow).

The basket begonia, *B. × t.* 'Pendula' has slender, cascading shoots. From June to September, it bears flowers 5–7.5 cm wide in a broad colour range, including rose-pink, scarlet and golden yellow.

The wax begonia, *Begonia semperflorens*, is a bushy plant that bears a mass of small flowers, 1.8–2.5 cm wide, in colours including white, pink and red, from June to late autumn. Its common name comes from the rounded, waxy, bright green leaves 5–10 cm long.

The elephant ear begonia, *Begonia haageana*, is a large plant that reaches 60–90 cm high and 60 cm wide. Its leaves are obliquely heart-shaped, hairy, 20 cm long, and deep green with purplish-red undersides. The pale pink flowers, 12–25 cm wide, are borne in summer.

The fuchsia begonia, *Begonia fuchsioides*, also grows up to 90 cm high and 60 cm wide. From late autumn to early spring, its bright pink or red flowers bloom amidst glossy, serrated, medium to deep green foliage.

BEGONIA × TUBERHYBRIDA
'JUDY LANGDON'
Large rose-like flowers.

BEGONIA
SEMPERFLORENS
Flowers white, pink or red.

BEGONIA FUCHSIOIDES
Flowers red or pink on long, pendulous stems.

SURVIVAL BASICS

Light and temperature: Bright, indirect sunlight; winter temperatures of 13–15 °C (55–59 °F).

Watering and feeding: Keep compost moist during flowering, but avoid continual saturation. When in flower, give a weak liquid fertilizer every 2 weeks.

Compost and repotting: Use peat-enriched compost. Transplant established tubers into pots 13 cm, then 20 cm, wide.

Propagation: Plant dormant tubers in boxes containing moist peat during March at 18 °C (64 °F).

WARNING: A dry atmosphere or compost causes flower buds to fall.

• Plant Identification p.13

A grey mould called botrytis forms on leaves and flowers if the air is damp and the temperature low. Improve air circulation, cut off infected parts and spray with a fungicide.

Leaves turn yellow if the plant is not getting enough light. Saturated or dry compost can also make the leaves lose their colour.

Leaves rot and turn pale yellow if the compost becomes waterlogged, especially in low winter temperatures.

Brown tips to the leaves result from an exceptionally dry atmosphere.

Begonia × tuberhybrida

PESTS AND DISEASES
Root knot eelworm
Weevils
Tarsonemid mites
Botrytis
Powdery mildew

• Pests pp.194–196   • Diseases p.197
• Checklists pp.212–217

IVY TREE

× *Fatshedera lizei*
Height: 1.2–1.8 m
Spread: 60–90 cm

This hybrid plant is a cross between two distinct genera: the false castor oil plant, *Fatsia japonica* 'Moseri', and the Irish ivy, *Hedera helix* 'Hibernica'. The × preceding the scientific name indicates a bigeneric hybrid (see glossary).

The leathery, five-lobed, shiny green leaves grow up to 20 cm wide on long stalks. When young, the plant has a central, upright stem; but with age it sprawls or climbs and needs the support of thin canes. To keep it bushy remove the growing tips.

Also recommended:
× *Fatshedera lizei* 'Variegata': Green leaves have cream edges and blotches.

Old plants lose their lower leaves. Take cuttings from the tops of the stems and leave the old plant to develop new shoots.

Cut back untidy shoots in spring or early summer to just above a leaf joint.

Leaves will drop in the dry atmosphere of centrally heated rooms. Provide humidity by standing the pot in a tray of moist pebbles.

Keep the leaves free from dust by wiping them with a soft, damp cloth.

SURVIVAL BASICS

Light and temperature: Bright, indirect sunlight, or light shade; winter temperatures of 5–7°C (41–45°F).
Watering and feeding: Water sparingly in winter; keep moist in summer. From spring to autumn, feed every 2 weeks with a weak liquid fertilizer.
Compost and repotting: Use John Innes potting compost No. 2. Repot in spring, usually every year.
Propagation: Take stem-tip cuttings in summer.

WARNING: Dull or shaded positions eventually lead to elongated stems and fewer leaves.

• Plant Identification p.20   • Propagation by Cuttings pp.176–178   • Checklists pp.212–217

FALSE CASTOR OIL PLANT

Fatsia japonica
Height: 0.9–1.2 m
Spread: 0.9–1.2 m

This quick-growing shrub can reach up to 10 m high when grown outdoors in warm areas. Indoors, it makes a small bushy plant with shiny, medium to deep green leaves on long stalks. Each leaf grows up to 25 cm across and has seven to nine, serrated, finger-like lobes, each with a pointed tip.

Mature plants grown outdoors may develop large heads of white flowers, formed from 4 cm-wide clusters, in late summer and early autumn. However, these are rarely seen on indoor plants.
Also recommended:
Fatsia japonica variegata: Slightly smaller; leaves have white edges to the lobes.

SURVIVAL BASICS

Light and temperature: Bright, indirect sunlight or light shade; winter temperature of 5°C (41°F).
Watering and feeding: Water sparingly in winter, but keep moist in summer. From spring to late summer, feed every 2 weeks with a weak liquid fertilizer.
Compost and repotting: Use John Innes potting compost No. 2. Repot in spring, when potbound, usually every year.
Propagation: Detach offshoots and pot up in spring.

WARNING: Strong sunlight and a dry atmosphere will cause the leaves to shrivel and fall off.

Yellowing leaves that eventually fall off are caused by high temperatures or a continually-saturated compost.

Long straggly shoots can be cut back to a leaf joint in spring.

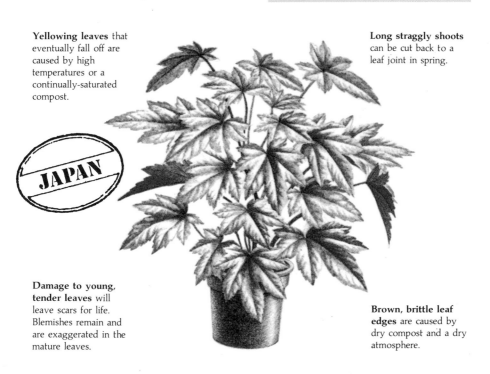

Damage to young, tender leaves will leave scars for life. Blemishes remain and are exaggerated in the mature leaves.

Brown, brittle leaf edges are caused by dry compost and a dry atmosphere.

• Plant Identification p.20   • Propagation by Offshoots   • Checklists pp.212–217
p.179

CYCLAMEN

Cyclamen persicum
Height: 15–30 cm
Spread: 15–35 cm

From late autumn to early spring, and especially at Christmas, millions of colourful flowering plants developed from this species are sold. They vary in height and come in colours including pink, white, red, purple and salmon. The flowers usually have five swept-back petals. They are 2.5–5 cm long and borne on 15–25 cm stalks. In cool conditions, they should remain in flower for two to three months. Store tubers in a cool place until late summer; then repot and water thoroughly to initiate growth.

The heart-shaped to rounded leaves, 5–7.5 cm wide, grow directly from the tuber beneath the potting mix on 10-cm stalks. The leaves cover the base of the plant and are often patterned or marbled in silver and green.

Many distinct varieties have been developed. Of the larger varieties, which grow to 23–30 cm, the most highly recommended is 'Rex', which has leaves prominently patterned in silver. 'Triumph' has large, abundant flowers in a wide colour range.

The 'Ruffled' hybrids have, as their name suggests, flowers with ruffled or fringed edges and are available in various shades of red. 'Decora' is famed for its attractive leaves and for the delicate pastel shades of its flowers. 'Grandia' has large, wavy, frilly-edged, salmon-pink flowers.

The smaller varieties, which grow 15–20 cm high, are usually scented. These include 'Puppet', 'Kaori', with attractive leaves and a distinct eye to its flowers, and 'Symphony', which can tolerate the rigours of central heating.

CYCLAMEN PERSICUM 'REX'
Leaves prominently patterned or marbled in silver.

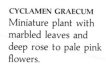

CYCLAMEN GRAECUM
Miniature plant with marbled leaves and deep rose to pale pink flowers.

CYCLAMEN PERSICUM 'ROSA VAN AALSMEER'
Petals frilly-edged.

SURVIVAL BASICS

Light and temperature: Bright, indirect sunlight; winter temperatures of 10–15 °C (50–59 °F).

Watering and feeding: Keep compost moist but not saturated. Apply a weak liquid fertilizer every 2 weeks in growing and flowering period.

Compost and repotting: Use John Innes potting compost No. 1. Repot when potbound.

Propagation: Sow seeds in late summer for flowering 15 months later.

WARNING: High temperatures, dry air and strong, direct sunlight reduce the flowering period and eventually kill the plant.

Stems and flowers will rot if water splashes on them repeatedly. Tubers, which are half-buried, also rot if water is poured on to them. Always water from below. Stand the pot in a saucer of water; remove it when moisture has percolated up to the surface.

Leaves turn yellow if the air is hot and dry. Dry compost and strong, direct sun can also cause yellowing. Keep the plant humid by standing the pot in a tray of wet pebbles or in a container of moist peat.

Soft, rotting flower stems should be removed at once. Twist and pull them off from their bases — do not leave a stump. Remove yellow or damaged leaves.

E. MED.

Cyclamen persicum

PESTS AND DISEASES
Cyclamen mites
Vine weevils
Aphids
Thrips
Botrytis

• Pests pp.194–196   • Diseases p.197
• Checklists pp.212–217

NORFOLK ISLAND PINE

Araucaria heterophylla
Height: 1.2–1.8 m
Spread: 45–75 cm

This slow-growing conifer reaches over 30 m high in its native Norfolk Island. In New Zealand it is used as a street tree. Indoors, it only grows to a height of 1.8 m at a rate of about 15 cm a year. Keeping it potbound restricts its growing even more. Fresh green growth produced in spring will darken the following autumn.

The pine has a symmetrical outline with tiered branches bearing dense clusters of slender needles 12 mm long. Once it reaches about 1.2 m in height, it starts to lose its lower branches and looks less attractive. It should then be replaced with a younger specimen.

The lower branches will eventually die in older plants. Cut the branch off at the main stem. Do not cut back the main stem itself, it will not produce new shoots.

Needles will fall in a hot, dry atmosphere. Water thoroughly but do not saturate the compost. Mist the branches on occasion.

In warm climates, the plant can stand outdoors on a sheltered patio in summer. Do not place it in strong, direct sunlight.

SURVIVAL BASICS

Light and temperature: Bright light in winter, and indirect sunlight in summer; winter temperature of 7°C (45°F).

Watering and feeding: Keep compost barely moist in winter; water more frequently in summer. Apply a weak liquid fertilizer every 2 weeks in summer.

Compost and repotting: Use John Innes potting compost No. 2. Repot in spring, when potbound, usually every 2–3 years.

Propagation: Sow seeds in spring or buy young plants.

WARNING: A hot dry atmosphere and dry compost cause needle drop.

• Plant Identification p.31
• Checklists pp.212–217

Commercial leaf-cleaning fluids will damage the leaves. To wash off dust and dirt, stand the palm under a warm but gentle shower.

Brown leaf tips are caused by a dry atmosphere. Cold draughts and dry compost in winter can also have the same effect.

Yellow leaves result from dry compost in summer. The older leaves are usually the first to suffer.

KENTIA PALM

Howeia forsteriana
Height: 1.8–3 m
Spread: 1.5–2.4 m

This long-lasting, single-stemmed palm, also sold as *Kentia forsteriana*, has dark green, arching fronds on leaf stalks up to 90 cm long. The leaflets are 2.5–3.5 cm wide, 15 cm long and held horizontally at about 2.5-cm intervals on the midrib of the frond.

The sentry palm, *Howeia belmoreana*, is almost identical to the kentia palm, except that its leaflets are more numerous and almost erect, its leaf stalks are shorter and the plant itself does not grow as quickly. Both plants are popular because they are the most tolerant of all the palms that will grow indoors.

PESTS AND DISEASES
Red spider mites
Mealy bugs
Scale insects

LORD
HOWE Is.

SURVIVAL BASICS

Light and temperature: Bright sunlight in winter, and indirect light in summer; winter temperatures of 10–12°C (50–54°F).

Watering and feeding: Keep compost barely moist in winter; water freely in summer. From April to September, add a weak liquid fertilizer every 2–3 weeks.

Compost and repotting: Use John Innes potting compost No. 2 or 3. Repot in spring, when potbound.

Propagation: Sow seeds in early spring.

WARNING: High winter temperatures, or hot, direct summer sunshine combined with dry air, are fatal.

• Plant Identification p.28   • Pests pp.194–196
• Palms pp.188–189   • Checklists pp.212–217

GLOXINIA

Sinningia speciosa
Height: 20–25 cm
Spread: 23–30 cm

The spectacular, velvety, bell-shaped flowers of gloxinia are produced between May and August. They are 5–7.5 cm long, 7.5 cm across and are borne on stiff stems above oblong to oval, velvety, fleshy, dark green leaves, up to 23 cm long. If gloxinia plants are bought when in bud, they should remain in flower for six to eight weeks.

Originally, gloxinias had purple or violet flowers, but now many other colours are available – some with plain-edged lobes to the flowers, others with frilly-edged lobes.

These varieties include 'Gregor Mendel' which grows 20 cm tall, with double, slightly ruffled, bright scarlet flowers edged in white. 'Satin Beauty Mixed' grows 23 cm tall. It has large flowers with frilly petals, some single-coloured, others flecked and spotted.

'Velvet Plush' grows 23 cm tall with rich, velvety, red flowers 7.5–10 cm wide. The popular 'Hetherset Hybrid' grows to 25 cm, and is available in a variety of bright colours.

'Multiflora Double Flowering Mixed' is 23 cm tall. More than half its flowers are double blooms in scarlet, soft rose, deep blue, lilac-blue or white, as well as bicolours.

'Freckle Face' also grows up to 23 cm tall. It has speckled or veined flowers in scarlet, carmine, pink, rose, purple or blue on a white background.

'Sutton's Mammoth Hybrid' is 23–25 cm high, with enormous bell-like flowers which are splashed or spotted in a wide colour range on a creamy-white background.

SINNINGIA SPECIOSA
'GREGOR MENDEL'
Double flowers are scarlet with white, ruffled edges.

SINNINGIA REGINA
Flowers violet and slipper-like with purple-spotted throats.

SINNINGIA PUSILLA
Miniature plant with violet, trumpet-shaped flowers.

SURVIVAL BASICS

Light and temperature: Bright, indirect sunlight; winter temperature of 18°C (64°F).

Watering and feeding: Keep compost moist. Feed with a weak liquid fertilizer every 10 days when in flower.

Compost and repotting: Use John Innes potting compost No. 2 or a peat-based type. Repot only when potbound.

Propagation: By seeds in February or March, or divide tubers in March.

WARNING: Wet, cold compost will eventually rot the plant's base.

• Plant Identification p.10

After flowering, the plant can be kept for blooming the following year. When the flowers begin to fade, place the plant in a cooler position and reduce the amount and frequency of watering. Remove dead flowers and leaves. In winter, store the tuberous roots at 10°C (50°F), and repot in fresh compost the following spring.

Flower buds will not open if the plant is in a cold draught or the atmosphere is dry.

Leaf tips curl and become brown if the atmosphere is too dry and the temperature exceptionally high. Stand the pot on a layer of pebbles in a shallow tray. Fill with just enough water to cover the pebbles.

Leaves become elongated and turn brown at their edges if the plant is placed in too shady a position.

Sinningia speciosa

PESTS AND DISEASES
Greenfly

• Pests pp.194–196
• Checklists pp.212–217

PARLOUR PALM

Chamaedorea elegans
Height: 45–75 cm
Spread: 45–60 cm

This is one of the most popular of all indoor palms. It takes several years to grow to its full height, but even then it is small compared with other palms. Each of its gently arching, yellowish leaf stalks grows 45–60 cm long and bears almost paired leaflets along the length of its midrib. These leaflets are narrow, tapering, lance-shaped and deep green, growing up to 20 cm long and 2 cm wide.

When the plant matures, and if it has been kept in good light, it bears insignificant, yellow flowers in small clusters followed by tiny, round, black fruits about 6 mm across.

Old leaves turn brown and droop. Cut them off cleanly with sharp secateurs.

Leaves turn yellow, especially in summer, if the compost is dry.

Leaf tips turn brown if the air is dry. In summer, mist the leaves daily.

SURVIVAL BASICS

Light and temperature: Bright, indirect sunlight in winter, light shade in summer; winter temperature of 12°C (54°F).

Watering and feeding: Keep the compost barely moist in winter; water freely in summer. In summer, apply a weak liquid fertilizer every 2–3 weeks.

Compost and repotting: Use John Innes potting compost No. 1 or 2. Repot in spring, when potbound.

Propagation: Sow seeds in spring.

WARNING: Avoid strong, direct summer sunlight.

PESTS
Red spider mites
Scale insects
Mealy bugs

CANARY DATE PALM

Phoenix canariensis
Height: 1.2–1.8 m
Spread: 0.9–1.5 m

This popular palm grows to 15 m in its native Canary Islands, but indoors will only reach about a tenth of this height. Its stiffly arching stalks are covered with slender, spiky, medium green leaflets that vary considerably in length. Short ones grow near the tip and the base of each stalk while longer ones grow from the middle.

The pygmy date palm, *Phoenix roebelenii*, sometimes known as the miniature date palm, is almost stemless and grows 0.9–1.2 m high. It has a crown of arching fronds, each composed of leaflets that bend downward at the tip.

Lower fronds turn brown as the palm ages. Do not rip them off; cut them off cleanly with sharp secateurs.

Leaf tips turn brown if the air is too dry in summer. Mist the palm regularly.

Lower fronds turn yellow in summer if the compost dries out. Keep it moist.

PESTS AND DISEASES
Red spider mites
Scale insects
Mealy bugs

SURVIVAL BASICS

Light and temperature: Bright, indirect sunlight; winter temperature of 10°C (50°F).

Watering and feeding: Keep compost barely moist in winter; water freely in summer. From April to September, apply a weak liquid fertilizer every 2–3 weeks.

Compost and repotting: Use John Innes potting compost No. 2. Repot in spring, when potbound.

Propagation: Divide and repot large congested plants in spring.

WARNING: A dry atmosphere, particularly if combined with strong sunlight, can be fatal.

• Plant Identification p.28   • Propagation by Division p.179   • Palms pp.188–189   • Pests pp.194–196   • Checklists pp.212–217

CINERARIA

Senecio cruentus
Height: 30–75 cm – see text
Spread: 25–45 cm

From late winter and through the spring, cinerarias bear large, domed heads of daisy-like flowers 1.8–7.5 cm wide. They come in a range of colours – some of them striking for their brilliance and intensity – that include blue, mauve, lavender, pink, red, white or mixtures of these.

In, the flowering period, which can last from four to six weeks, the flower heads conceal the array of leaves below almost completely. The leaves are roughly heart-shaped, soft, jagged-edged, dark green and up to 20 cm wide.

Cinerarias are available in several distinct forms. The hybrid 'Grandiflora' is 45 cm tall, with large, broad-petalled blooms that are 5–7.5 cm wide. Double-flowered varieties grow 30–45 cm tall with blooms 5 cm wide. 'Multiflora Nana' forms are 30–38 cm high, with flowers 2.5–5 cm wide. The 'Stellata' forms grow to 38–75 cm, are more branched and have star-shaped, thin-petalled flowers 2.5–4 cm wide.

Other plants in the same genus may also be grown as houseplants. Many are totally different from cinerarias in size and shape. The string of beads, *Senecio rowleyanus*, has succulent, rounded, bluish-green leaves 6 mm wide and clustered around slender, creeping stems that can trail to 75 cm. Each bead-like leaf has a transparent band and a tiny, pointed tip. In autumn, sweetly-scented, white, brush-like flowers appear.

The German ivy, *Senecio mikanioides*, has green, semi-succulent leaves that are 5–6 cm wide, 5–6 cm long and have five to seven pointed lobes. The variegated form has yellow blotches on the leaves.

MULTIFLORA NANA
Compact plants with flowers in single or mixed colours.

DOUBLE
Compact plants with flowers either double or semi-double in a wide colour range.

STELLATA
Branching plants with thin-petalled flowers.

SURVIVAL BASICS

Light and temperature: Bright, but not direct sunlight; winter temperatures of 7–13°C (45–55°F).

Watering and feeding: Keep compost moist, especially in the flowering period. Feed every 10–14 days, as soon as flower buds are formed.

Compost and repotting: Use John Innes potting compost No. 1 or 2; pot on young plants into progressively larger pots.

Propagation: Sow seeds in summer in loam-based compost at 13°C (55°F).

WARNING: Waterlogged compost causes cinerarias to collapse and die.

• Plant Identification p.9

A short flowering
period is the result of
high temperatures and
dry compost.
Temperatures over
15°C (59°F) will soon
kill this plant.

Plants wilt if the
compost is dry. Both
the flowers and soft
leaves are affected.
Stand the pot in a
bucket of water until
air bubbles cease to
rise from the surface
of the compost.

The roots will rot if
the rootball becomes
totally saturated.
Remove the pot to
allow the roots to dry
out. Wrap several
layers of newspaper
around the rootball to
help speed up the
process.

Yellowing, wilting
foliage is caused by
cold draughts,
especially if the
compost is dry.

Senecio cruentus
'Grandiflora

PESTS AND DISEASES
Greenfly
Whitefly
Leaf miners
Thrips
Botrytis

• Pests pp.194–196   • Diseases p.197
• Checklists pp.212–217

MAIDENHAIR FERN

Adiantum capillus-veneris
Height: 15–25 cm
Spread: 15–25 cm

This delicate-looking fern has graceful fronds that grow on blackish-brown, wiry stalks. They are composed of triangular lobed leaflets on arching fronds. The fronds may grow as long as 60 cm and as wide as 25 cm, while the leaflets may reach 2.5 cm across.

The delta maidenhair, *Adiantum raddianum*, grows 30–45 cm tall with a spread of 38–60 cm. Its purple-black stems bear graceful, triangular-shaped, pale green fronds that are 15 cm wide and 20 cm long.

Also recommended:
A. r. 'Fragrantissimum': Dense foliage has a strong fragrance.

SURVIVAL BASICS

Light and temperature: Indirect sunlight in winter, light shade in summer; winter temperature of 7°C (45°F).

Watering and feeding: Keep compost moist at all times, but not waterlogged. From April to September, add a weak liquid fertilizer every 2 weeks.

Compost and repotting: Use peat-based compost, or John Innes potting compost No. 1 with extra peat. Repot in spring, when potbound.

Propagation: Divide and repot congested plants in spring.

WARNING: Do not position the fern too close to, or above, a radiator.

Fronds that turn pale yellow, even though the plant is in the shade, need regular feeding, especially in the active growing period.

Fronds die back and wither if either the compost or the air become too dry. Lightly mist the fronds and thoroughly soak the compost.

The delicate fronds turn pale in strong sunlight, especially in summer. They are soon scorched, causing them to turn brown and wither.

PESTS AND DISEASES
Wood lice
Root mealy bugs

If the fronds wilt and the compost is dry, stand the pot in a bowl of water until moisture seeps to the surface. Then remove and allow excess water to drain off.

TEMPERATE ZONES

• Plant Identification p.16   • Ferns pp.186–187
• Propagation by Division p.179

• Pests pp.194–196
• Checklists pp.212–217

LADDER FERN

Nephrolepis exaltata
Height: 45–75 cm
Spread: 60–90 cm, or more

The pale green fronds of this popular indoor fern grow from a short, thick stem which is actually the top of a half-covered upright rhizome. Each frond is composed of numerous leaflets that grow alternately from either side of the midrib.

The Boston fern, *N. exaltata* 'Bostoniensis', comes from North America and is the variety most usually grown. Its cascades of feathery, tapering fronds grow up to 90 cm long.

Also recommended:
N. e. 'Hillii': Has crinkled, light green fronds that cascade freely.
N. e. 'Marshallii': Has densely-crested, pale green, semi-upright fronds.

SURVIVAL BASICS

Light and temperature: Indirect sunlight in winter, diffused and lightly shaded in summer; winter temperature of 10°C (50°F).
Watering and feeding: Keep compost moist, but not waterlogged. From April to September, add a weak liquid fertilizer every 2–3 weeks.
Compost and repotting: Use peat-based compost, or John Innes potting compost No. 1 with extra peat. Repot in spring, when potbound.
Propagation: In spring, divide and repot congested plants.

WARNING: Strong sunlight and a dry atmosphere are fatal. A cool position is essential in summer.

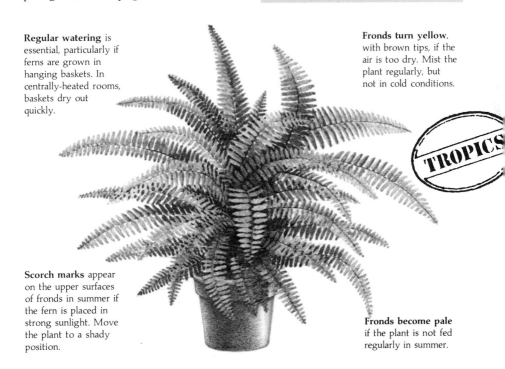

Regular watering is essential, particularly if ferns are grown in hanging baskets. In centrally-heated rooms, baskets dry out quickly.

Fronds turn yellow, with brown tips, if the air is too dry. Mist the plant regularly, but not in cold conditions.

Scorch marks appear on the upper surfaces of fronds in summer if the fern is placed in strong sunlight. Move the plant to a shady position.

Fronds become pale if the plant is not fed regularly in summer.

TROPICS

• Plant Identification p.17   • Propagation by Division p.179   • Ferns pp.186–187
• Checklists pp.212–217

RAT'S TAIL CACTUS

Aporocactus flagelliformis
Height: 7.5 cm
Spread: 15–25 cm, then trailing

This cascading cactus has stems that are 12 mm thick and grow up to 90 cm long. They are medium green, ribbed and covered with short, brownish spines. During April and May, they bear funnel-shaped, pink or magenta flowers that are 7.5 cm long. These rise from the top of the plant, as well as from along the stems.

A hybrid, with the rat's tail cactus as one of its parents, is sometimes available. Its naming is rather confused: it is listed as either *Heliaporus smithii* or *Aporocactus mallisonii*. Its bright green stems are slightly thicker, shorter, more deeply ribbed and longer-spined than those of *A. flagelliformis*. The red, cup-shaped flowers are larger, but fewer in number.

Two other unusual, but distinctive, cascading cacti are recommended as houseplants. The mistletoe cactus, *Rhipsalis baccifera*, better known as *Rhipsalis cassytha*, trails to 9 m in South America, Sri Lanka and Africa where it hangs from trees in its jungle habitat. Indoors, however, it is much shorter. The greenish, cylindrical, branching stems grow up to 1.2 m long and up to 5 mm wide. In summer, they bear greenish-white flowers 6 mm wide, followed by tiny, white berries that resemble the fruit of mistletoe.

The chain cactus or link plant, *Lepismium paradoxum*, often sold as *Rhipsalis paradoxa*, trails to 90 cm with three- to four-angled, fleshy stems that may be 12–18 mm thick. These are twisted, with joints every 2.5–5 cm. Another branching cactus, *Rhipsalis cereuscula*, has rounded, bright green stems up to 40 cm long with short side branches from which tiny, greenish flowers appear.

APOROPHYLLUM 'MAIDEN'S BLUSH' Hybrid between aporocactus and epiphyllum. Flowers pale pink on short stems.

APOROCACTUS MALLISONII Red flowers on shorter, stiffer, more deeply-ribbed stems than *A. flagelliformis*.

SURVIVAL BASICS

Light and temperature: Bright, indirect sunlight; winter temperatures of 7–10°C (45–50°F).

Watering and feeding: Keep compost moist, especially in the flowering period. Add a weak liquid fertilizer during flowering, until late summer.

Compost and repotting: Use John Innes potting compost No. 2, with extra peat. Repot in spring, when potbound, usually every year.

Propagation: Take cuttings from late spring to midsummer.

WARNING: Make sure the compost is rich and moist when the cactus is in flower.

• Plant Identification p.12

Water with clean rainwater in hardwater areas.

Roots will decay and rot if winter temperatures are too high and the compost becomes waterlogged.

MEXICO

Aporocactus flagelliformis

Long, trailing stems are vulnerable, so position the plant where it will not be damaged by people passing by. Flowers are soon spoilt if knocked, as are the stems which are brittle in winter.

Flowers quickly wilt and shrivel if the compost dries out. Hanging baskets are particularly hazardous in this respect. Check the compost every other day in the flowering period to make sure it has not dried out.

PESTS AND DISEASES
Mealy bugs
Root mealy bugs
Red spider mites

- Propagation by Cuttings pp.176–178
- Cacti and Succulents pp.184–185
- Pests pp.194–196
- Checklists pp.212–217

SILVER LACE FERN

Pteris ensiformis 'Victoriae'
Height: 30–38 cm
Spread: 25–30 cm

This small, attractive fern has slender, upright or arching, triangular, green fronds with silvery-white variegations on their centres. The true species, *Pteris ensiformis*, has slender, deep green fronds, and is slightly larger.

The ribbon fern, *Pteris cretica*, has slightly serrated, light green fronds borne on wiry, upright stems. The variegated table fern, *P. c.* 'Albolineata', has a white band along each leaf, while *P. c.* 'Wimsetti' has crested edges.

Also recommended:
Pteris quadriaurita argyraea: Has long, deeply-lobed, grey-green fronds with whitish-green bands on their centres.

SURVIVAL BASICS

Light and temperature: Indirect light in winter, light shade in summer; winter temperature of 13°C (55°F).

Watering and feeding: Keep compost barely moist in winter; water freely in summer. From April to September, add a weak liquid fertilizer every 2–3 weeks.

Compost and repotting: Use equal parts peat, sharp sand and loam. Repot in spring, when potbound.

Propagation: Divide and repot congested plants in spring.

WARNING: Direct, strong sunlight and a dry atmosphere soon cause the fronds to shrivel.

N. INDIA–AUSTRALIA

Fronds shrivel and die if the compost or air is dry. Mist the foliage and thoroughly soak the compost.

Fronds shrivel, turn pale and their edges turn brown if the compost is dry. If necessary, stand the pot in a bucket of water until moisture seeps to the surface. Remove and allow excess water to drain.

Limp, pale fronds are probably due to lack of food. Feed the plant regularly throughout the summer, and repot into a larger pot in spring if the compost is congested with roots.

- Plant Identification p.27
- Propagation by Division p.179
- Ferns pp.186–187
- Checklists pp.212–217

BIRD'S NEST FERN

Asplenium nidus
Height: 0.6–1 m
Spread: 30–60 cm

This popular fern has glossy, apple-green, strap-like fronds that grow up like the feathers on a large shuttlecock. Each frond has a brown midrib and can grow to 60 cm long and 7,5–13 cm wide. New fronds unfurl from the dark brown base; they are delicate and easily damaged.

The hen and chicken fern, *Asplenium bulbiferum*, looks entirely different, with finely-cut, feathery, medium green fronds reminiscent of carrot-tops. Mature plants reach 45–60 cm high and 60–90 cm wide. Bulbils (leafy plantlets) grow on the upper surfaces of the fronds, especially at the edges. These can be rooted by pegging a frond on to compost.

SURVIVAL BASICS

Light and temperature: Bright, indirect sunlight in winter, light shade in summer; winter temperature of 13°C (55°F).

Watering and feeding: Keep compost barely moist in winter; water freely in summer. From April to September, give a weak liquid fertilizer every 2–3 weeks.

Compost and repotting: Use John Innes potting compost No. 2 with extra peat. Repot in spring, when potbound.

Propagation: Sow spores in spring.

WARNING: High temperatures and a dry atmosphere make the fronds shrivel.

Brown, crisp leaf edges are caused by compost that has been allowed to dry out. Keep the compost moist in summer.

INDIA–AUSTRALIA

Scale insects are the fern's worst enemy. They usually appear on the undersides of the fronds. When young, wipe them off with a damp cloth; but colonies must be sprayed with a suitable chemical.

PESTS AND DISEASES
Woodlice
Scale insects
Slugs

• Plant Identification p.21   • Pests pp.194–196
• Ferns pp.186–187   • Checklists pp.212–217

EASTER CACTUS

Rhipsalidopsis gaertneri
Height: 15–25 cm
Spread: 45–75 cm, trailing

This spreading, cascading, jungle cactus has fleshy, flat, dull green stems with notched, shallowly-scalloped edges. The stems may have three to six edges, even though they appear to be flat.

The cactus bears trumpet-shaped, pendulous, bright red flowers 4–6 cm wide with sharply-pointed petals. Although individual flowers are short-lived – they last for about four days – the flowering period lasts several weeks, usually from late winter to early spring.

The crab cactus, *Schlumbergera truncata*, also has nearly flat stems, with joints every 5–7.5 cm. The bright green stems become tinged with red as they mature and have two to four deeply-cut notches on each side. From November to January, it produces 5–7.5 cm-long flowers in shades of crimson, purple, blue or lilac, as well as white. Some of the petals are swept back. It is often erroneously known as the Christmas cactus.

The true Christmas cactus, *Schlumbergera × buckleyi*, is a cross between *S. russelliana* and *S. truncata*. The fleshy, medium green stems are flat, with rounded indentations at their edges. Each segment is about 5 cm long. The magenta or rose-coloured flowers are 5–7.5 cm long and appear over the Christmas period, from December to February.

Hybrids of the closely-related orchid cactus, *Epiphyllum × ackermannii*, are widely grown. They have flattened or triangular stems which are wavy-edged or notched and grow upright to 75 cm. The showy flowers appear in May or June. They are 10–13 cm across, in scarlet, white or yellow, some heavily scented.

SCHLUMBERGERA
× BUCKLEYI
Magenta or rose
flowers appear at
Christmas time.

RHIPSALIDOPSIS ROSEA
Rose-pink flowers
appear in early spring.

SURVIVAL BASICS

Light and temperature: Bright sunlight in winter, indirect light in summer; winter temperatures of 13–15 °C (55–59 °F).

Watering and feeding: Keep compost moist, but not saturated. During flowering and until late summer, feed every 2 weeks.

Compost and repotting: Use John Innes potting compost No. 1 with a handful of peat and sharp sand. Repot in spring, when potbound.

Propagation: Take stem cuttings in summer.

WARNING: Do not leave the plant in high temperatures in summer.

• Plant Indentification p.12

BRAZIL

The flat stems easily collect dust. Gently wipe them clean with a soft cloth. If flower buds are forming, take special care not to dislodge them.

Flowers fail to form if the compost is too wet. Keep it barely moist in late winter to encourage flowering.

Allow young stems to harden in summer by placing the cactus outdoors but out of direct sunlight.

Flowers soon wilt and shrivel if the compost dries out.

Rhipsalidopsis gaertneri

PESTS AND DISEASES
Mealy bugs

• Propagation by Cuttings pp.176–178
• Cacti and Succulents pp.184–185
• Pests pp.194–196
• Checklists pp.212–217

BURRO'S TAIL

Sedum morganianum
Height: 5–7.5 cm
Spread: 15–20 cm, then trailing

The trailing stems of this succulent are formed of fleshy, cylindrical, waxy, grey-green leaf segments up to 18 mm long. The stems can trail as much as 90 cm when the plant is grown in a hanging basket. Clusters of pale pink flowers may be borne at the ends of the stems from June to September.

Sedum sieboldii 'Medio-variegatum' spreads up to 40 cm and trails up to 25 cm when grown in a hanging basket. The pliable stems bear flat, light grey, attractively blotched leaves with pinkish-white edges. Clusters of pink flowers may appear in autumn at the ends of the trailing stems.

SURVIVAL BASICS

Light and temperature: Bright sunlight; winter temperatures of 7–10°C (45–50°F).

Watering and feeding: Keep compost barely moist in winter; water freely in summer, adding a weak liquid fertilizer every 3 weeks.

Compost and repotting: Use John Innes potting compost No. 1, with extra loam. Repot in spring, when potbound.

Propagation: Divide congested plants in spring, or take leaf cuttings in early summer.

WARNING: Do not use rich compost, since this encourages lush growth at the expense of flowers.

The small, succulent leaves are easily detached. Handle the plant with great care and position it away from passing people or animals.

Roots will rot in a cold, wet compost. If winter temperatures are below the recommended minimum, allow the compost to dry out between waterings.

Leaves turn pale and wilt if the compost is kept too wet in winter. If the compost becomes totally saturated, remove the pot and allow the rootball to dry out.

Leaves fall off suddenly if very cold water is used in winter. Too dry a compost will have the same effect.

PESTS AND DISEASES
Mealy bugs
Greenfly

• Plant Identification p.15   • Propagation by Cuttings pp.176–178   • Propagation by Division p.179   • Pests pp.194–196   • Checklists pp.212–217

SILK OAK

Grevillea robusta
Height: 0.9–1.8 m
Spread: 38–45 cm

Roots will rot if the compost is wet while the plant is kept in a cool room in winter. If the recommended temperature cannot be achieved, keep the compost slightly drier.

Leaves scorch and turn brown if the plant is kept in strong sunlight in summer.

Broken branches will spoil the pleasing symmetry of mature specimens. Position the plant where its foliage cannot be damaged.

This quick-growing evergreen becomes a large tree in its native Australia, where its prettily-marked timber is widely used in making furniture. As a houseplant, it will reach its maximum height within about five years.

The spreading, medium to deep green leaves resemble the fronds of a feathery fern. Their upper surfaces are downy while their undersides are covered in silky hairs. The orange-red flowers are seldom produced by plants grown indoors.

The silk oak can be cut back to produce a bushy plant, though many people consider taller plants to be more elegant and attractive.

SURVIVAL BASICS

Light and temperature: Bright sunlight in winter, diffused in summer; winter temperatures of 4–7°C (39–45°F).

Watering and feeding: Keep compost barely moist in winter; water freely in summer. From May to September, add a weak liquid fertilizer every 2 weeks.

Compost and repotting: Use John Innes potting compost No. 2. Repot in spring, when potbound, usually every other year.

Propagation: Sow seeds in spring.

WARNING: The fern-like appearance of the leaves coarsens and thickens as the plant ages.

• Plant Identification p.31
• Checklists pp.212–217

CARE AND CULTIVATION

Although your home provides plants with warmth and shelter, it remains an unnatural environment. The effects of central heating, the variability in light intensity, the absence of rain, the presence of draughts, fumes and aerosol sprays — all these conspire against a plant's wellbeing.

Yet plants are adaptable, though to varying degrees. Most will tolerate the artificial conditions of your home for a short while, but they need to be provided with regular care and attention if they are to survive — and flourish — for more than a few weeks.

Plants require light, water, nutrients, air (often humid air) and a particular temperature range in order to survive and grow. They vary widely in the quantity and quality of these requirements — desert cacti, for example, need plenty of light and heat, whereas ferns need partial or light shade and high humidity. (See Plants in Profile [pp.32–145] for details of the requirements of specific plants.)

The Care and Cultivation section that follows outlines all aspects of growing and looking after houseplants, from choosing and buying plants to explaining the principles behind their requirements; and from pots, composts and the techniques of repotting to plant grooming and vacation care. A box feature on each aspect of plant maintenance summarizes the important points to remember in each instance.

Inexpensive and rewarding ways of increasing your favourite and most flourishing houseplants are clearly explained on pp.176–181. These include propagation techniques such as stem and leaf cuttings, division, air-layering, seeds and offsets.

Special features on groups of plants that generally require special attention are provided on pp.182–193. The groups featured are bulbs, ferns, cacti and succulents, palms, bromeliads, orchids and insect-eating plants.

The section ends with details of the common pests and diseases that are likely to infect and infest your plants. Each pest and disease mentioned in the Plants in Profile section (pp.32–145) is illustrated; descriptions and recommended ways of treating them are given alongside each.

Cross references, mainly to other pages in the Care and Cultivation section, are provided at the bottom of each page. If you wish to know more about particular plants which are mentioned, you are recommended to use one of the indexes (pp.218–224).

Choosing the right plant for the right place requires thought and planning. You need first to ascertain a plant's needs and whether or not your home offers an environment in which it will thrive. If you are an absolute beginner, start by buying plants noted for their resilience and requiring little attention. Do not, in the first flush of enthusiasm, go overboard and purchase anything that takes your fancy.

Look at your home from a plant's point of view. Do you have light or shady rooms, central heating, draughts, animals, children? Do you have much time to devote to plants? These are all important factors to consider before making a purchase. You cannot, for instance, expect cacti to thrive in the shade or aloes to withstand draughts; floorstanding plants cannot defend themselves against passing dogs or children; and maidenhair ferns will not put up with your neglect.

Always buy plants from reputable retailers or garden centres who you know have the plants' best interests at heart. You can usually tell at a glance whether a plant has been well cared for. Remember it is always worth paying for quality — if you buy a diseased plant, it could endanger your whole collection.

WHEN BUYING PLANTS . . .
- Buy from a reputable retailer or garden centre.
- Avoid plants displayed outside shops, especially in winter. Both compost and plant will be so chilled that the plant will probably collapse and die once you bring it into the warmth of your home.
- Do not buy plants that show signs of pests and/or disease.
- Do not buy plants with long, bare stems or those unevenly clothed with leaves.
- Check the bottom of the pot. If roots are growing through the drainage holes, the plant is almost certainly potbound — don't buy it.
- Do not buy plants which have green slime on the surface of the compost or on the pot. This is a sign of overwatering.
- Make sure flowering plants have plenty of healthy-looking buds still waiting to open.
- Make sure the plant is clearly identified.
- Do not buy plants with damaged, wilting or fallen leaves.
- Check that the compost is moist — plants in a dry compost may be weak.
- Avoid plants obviously too large or too small for their pots.
- Remember that a cheap plant that dies within a few days is an expensive purchase.
- Remember to protect your newly-purchased plants while taking them home.
- Make sure you acclimatize new plants to the conditions of your home (see p.149).

TAKING PLANTS HOME
- If you must buy houseplants, especially winter-flowering ones, on cold, windy days, make sure they have a good protective wrapping.
- Buy plants last on shopping expeditions to avoid damaging them while carrying them, or having to leave them too long in the car.
- Do not keep plants in the boot of your car in cold or hot weather – they will either freeze or bake.
- Prop plants up in a box to prevent them falling over in the car.

ACCLIMATIZING PLANTS TO THEIR NEW HOME
- When you first get a plant home, keep it in a fairly cool room, out of draughts and direct sunlight.
- Keep the compost just moist; do not overwater.
- After 10–14 days, move it to its permanent position. Flowering plants can be put in their permanent positions at once.
- Mist the plant regularly.
- If a leaf or flower falls off, it does not mean your plant is dying.

A HEALTHY HOUSEPLANT

Stems erect and sturdy. Avoid plants with wilting stems or stems showing signs of mildew. Check the base of a plant for signs of stem rot.

Leaves sturdy and robust. Avoid plants with leaves turning brown at the edges or leaves already yellow. Blotchy, mottled, mouldy or curling leaves indicate an infection.

Buds firm and healthy. Avoid plants with black buds or shrivelled, distorted buds caused by a virus or pests.

Flowers vigorous with good colour. Avoid plants with wilting or blotched blooms which result from lack of feeding.

Examine the undersides of leaves for signs of insect infestation.

• Watering pp.158–161   • Pests and Diseases pp.194–197   • Checklists pp.212–217

Energy from light is essential for plants to survive. Light activates photosynthesis, a series of chemical reactions that take place in green leaves, by which plants produce their own food in the form of carbohydrates.

Plants vary widely in their requirements for light, just as they do for water, warmth and humidity. Some plants need plenty of bright, direct sunlight, while others need only shady, indirect light. Between these extremes, a broad range of light conditions will satisfy the needs of most of your houseplants.

A plant's need for light varies throughout the year. In its season of active growth, when it is putting out new leaves and perhaps flowers, it will need more intense light — and more hours of it — than in its dormant phase. This is why the active growth period for many plants coincides with the onset of spring and the longer periods of daylight.

Most plants need between 12 and 16 hours of light a day to maintain healthy growth. Many flowering plants need at

HOW PLANTS LIVE

Plants make their own food from sunlight, water and carbon dioxide taken in via tiny pores in the leaves. Essential to this process, a series of reactions called photosynthesis, are molecules of chlorophyll that give the leaves their green colour. Photosynthesis only takes place during the day, but plants breathe all the time, taking in oxygen and giving off carbon dioxide and water.

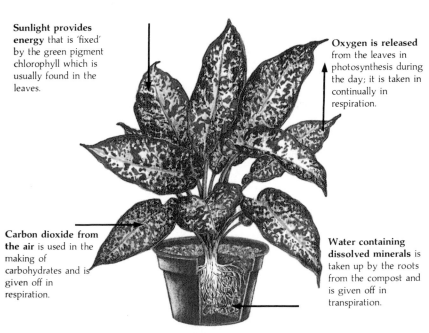

Sunlight provides energy that is 'fixed' by the green pigment chlorophyll which is usually found in the leaves.

Oxygen is released from the leaves in photosynthesis during the day; it is taken in continually in respiration.

Carbon dioxide from the air is used in the making of carbohydrates and is given off in respiration.

Water containing dissolved minerals is taken up by the roots from the compost and is given off in transpiration.

least 12 hours of light to activate flowering, while others only bloom when the light is restricted to fewer hours.

The natural reaction of plants is to grow toward a light source. This is called phototropism. When light comes from one direction only, a plant's stem will soon bend toward it and the leaves will turn to catch as much light as possible. To make sure your plant grows straight upward in these conditions, turn it round every few days (see below).

If light only comes from one direction, the plant's stem will bend that way. The pot must be turned to counteract unbalanced growth.

Do not turn the pot around and simply wait for the plant to bend back in the opposite direction – its growth will become distorted.

Mark the pot with an X to indicate the starting position and rotate the pot through 180° every few days. This will ensure even growth all round.

WHEN PROVIDING LIGHT, REMEMBER . . .

● Leaves, stems and flowers will grow toward a light source. If necessary, rotate your plants through 180° every few days to ensure balanced growth all round.

● Pale coloured walls and ceilings reflect light. Plants can benefit from this, especially in winter and in poorly-lit rooms.

● Keep plants close to windows in winter to allow them to catch as much natural light as possible. But beware of cold draughts.

● Flowering and growth are reduced when light is poor.

● Strong, direct sunlight soon scorches the leaves of most plants, except cacti and succulents. Net curtains help to reduce light intensity.

● Keep windows clean especially in winter to maximize the light falling on your plants.

● Open curtains early on bright summer mornings to make maximum use of the longer hours of light.

● Do not suddenly move a plant from a dull spot to one receiving direct sunlight, or vice versa.

● Variegated plants will lose the variegations on their leaves if kept in a shady position.

● Never splash water on leaves exposed to strong sunlight. Water droplets act like lenses, focusing the sun's rays which burn the leaves.

● In poor light, leaves are small and pale. Lower leaves turn yellow, dry at the edges and then fall off.

● Watering pp.158–161
● Feeding pp.162–163

Providing the right light for your plants means being selective about where you position them. Your choices of natural light will be dictated by which way your windows face.

The amount and quality of natural light entering a room varies with the time of day, the season and your geographical location. In summer, south-facing windows provide long hours of bright light, while windows facing east receive the less powerful rays of the morning sun. West-facing windows prolong a plant's day, while the light received in north-facing rooms is gentle and even.

Do not assume that simply because a room appears bright and sunny all parts of it will be receiving the same amount of light. In fact, light intensity decreases dramatically as the distance from a bright, sunny window increases. Thus, plants placed 2.4 m away will receive only 5—10 per cent of the light available on the windowsill. Most plants prefer bright positions without full sun, about 2 m from a sunny window.

LIGHT REQUIREMENTS

PLANTS FOR BRIGHT, SUNNY WINDOWS:	PLANTS FOR SOME DIRECT, BUT NOT FULL, SUN:	PLANTS FOR BRIGHT, BUT NOT FULL; SUN:	PLANTS FOR SEMI-SHADE:
Amaryllis	African violet	Aluminium plant	Chinese evergreen
Burro's tail	Busy lizzie	Bromeliads	False castor oil plant
Easter cactus	Chrysanthemum	Cast iron plant (below)	Ferns
Partridge-breasted aloe	Croton	Common Ivy	Ivy tree
Pelargonium	Mother-in-law's	Cyclamen	Painted net leaf
Rat's tail cactus	tongue	False aralia	Piggy-back plant
Tree aloe (below)	Pink jasmine	Painter's palette	Prayer plant
	(below)	Philodendrons	Sweetheart plant
	Poinsettia	Swiss cheese plant	(below)
	Rubber plant		
	Shrimp plant		
	Spider plant		
	Wandering Jew		

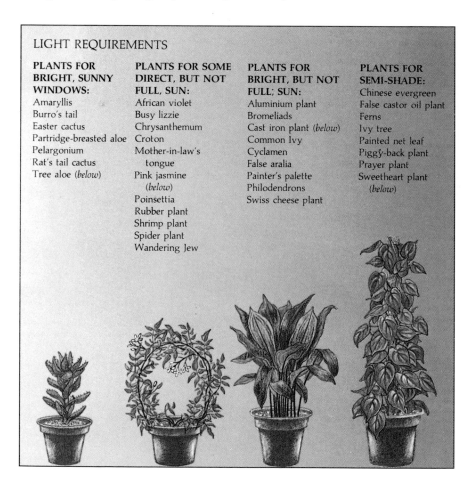

The fluorescent tubes
should, in general, be
positioned 30–60 cm
above foliage plants
and 15–30 cm above
flowering plants. If
possible, purchase or
make a unit in which
the distance between
plants and light source
can be adjusted.

INDOOR LIGHT GARDENS

You can transform dull rooms and brighten up any dark and gloomy corners by installing an indoor light garden. Fluorescent tubes, which provide plants with the light energy they need, give you an opportunity to have African violets flowering all year round and pelargoniums blooming in the winter.

Other plants that will thrive under artificial, fluorescent light include peperomias, gloxinias, marantas, calceolarias, cinerarias, begonias and bromeliads.

You can buy a simple, ready-made unit such as the one illustrated above. It consists of a trough for plants, above which is suspended a reflective hood with fluorescent tubes. If you want to build your own unit, it is best to ask a qualified electrician to install the lights.

Most plants need at least 12 hours of light each day of their growing season. Many plants 'know' how many hours of daylight there are and they respond with flowers or growth when the day reaches a critical length.

Growing plants under artificial light can be an exact science. Find out how much light individual plants will need and how far to place them from the tubes. For example, hot water plants need 12–16 hours of light and should be placed 10 cm from the tubes; begonias need 16–18 hours and should be placed 7.5 cm away.

Remember that indoor light gardens must be regularly maintained. The fluorescent tubes will need to be renewed and the hood must be kept clean. In addition, the height of the hood will have to be adjusted as the plants grow to keep the lights at a fixed distance from them.

As a general rule, if the plants are too near the lights, their leaves will curl; if too far away, their stems will grow lanky. Do not forget to water the plants regularly. And install a time switch to ensure the plants receive 8–10 hours of darkness each day.

• Lighting pp.208–209
• Checklists pp.212–217

During their active growth period, most houseplants will thrive in the warm conditions that prevail in most modern homes. When they are dormant, usually during winter, their need for warmth will be less.

The preferred minimum night temperature ranges for many of the plants included in the Plants in Profile section (pp.32–145) are shown in the chart opposite. Four ranges are described: cool, mild, moderate and warm. Some plants flourish in more than one range; these are indicated by symbols. However, the majority of houseplants will perish if they are left for too long at temperatures outside their preferred range.

Most plants will tolerate the ambient temperature in centrally-heated homes as long as they are provided with sufficient humidity. The maximum temperature which they can comfortably tolerate – assuming they receive the extra humidity – is about 29.5°C (85°F).

For a growing houseplant, air temperature goes hand in hand with light intensity and humidity. The warmer the air becomes, the quicker a plant uses up energy. If the quality and quantity of light are good, and the humidity adequate, the plant will flourish. If not, the plant will use up its stores of food quicker than it can replace them.

Dramatic temperature changes can be most damaging. While many plants can tolerate temperatures just outside their preferred range, they do not like sudden or significant changes. For example, plants will accept a drop from a daytime 15.5°C (60°F) to 10°C (50°F) at night; but they will suffer if the temperature falls from 15.5°C (60°F) to 4.5°C (40°F).

WHEN PROVIDING WARMTH, REMEMBER . . .

● Balance air temperature with light and humidity. The more warmth you give, the more light and, especially, the more humidity your plants will need. As a general rule, hot, dry air is fatal but hot, humid air is acceptable.

● Water plants more often in warm rooms, less in cold rooms. Plants may be able to tolerate colder conditions than they would normally prefer if the compost is kept on the dry side.

● Remove plants from cold windowsills in winter, especially if they are positioned between windows and curtains. This rule does not apply to double-glazed nor to secondary windows.

● Keep plants out of through draughts, away from ill-fitting doors and windows, and the cold currents generated by air conditioners.

● Keep plants away from hot radiators in winter.

● Keep hot spotlights away from leaves and flowers to prevent burning them.

● Move plants to a cooler room when they are in their dormant phase. At the same time, give them less water.

● If the air is too warm, flowers will fade quickly; lower leaves will wilt, their edges will turn brown and eventually they will fall off.

● If the air is too cold, leaves will curl, turn brown and fall off.

● Sudden or significant changes in air temperature will cause leaves to turn yellow and fall off.

HOUSEPLANT TEMPERATURE GUIDE

5°F
4°C

5°F
5°C

5°F
3°C

45°F
7°C

35°F
.5°C

Warm **18.5–24°C** **(65–75 F):**	■ Angel's tears ■ Blushing bromeliad Earth star False aralia Flaming sword Pineapple plant Scarlet star	■ Urn plant	
Moderate **13–18.5°C** **(55–65 F):**	African violet Amaryllis ▲ Azalea ▲ Boat lily Busy lizzie Chinese evergreen Croton ▲ Cyclamen	▲ Dragon tree Dumb cane Easter cactus Gloxinia Goldfish plant Hot water plant Hyacinth Painted net leaf	Peacock plant Persian violet Poinsettia Polka dot plant Rose of China Rubber plant
Mild **7–13 C** **(45–55 F):**	Asparagus fern Bird's nest fern Chrysanthemum Cineraria Fairy primrose Hydrangea Kangaroo vine Kentia palm	Ladder fern ■ Mother-in-law's tongue ■ Parasol plant ■ Peace lily Pelargonium Pink jasmine Shrimp plant	Spider plant Swiss cheese plant
Cool **1.5–7 C** **(35–45 F):**	Canary Island ivy ▲ Cast iron plant False castor oil plant Ivy tree ▲ Maidenhair fern Norfolk Island pine Partridge-breasted aloe	Piggy-back plant Silk oak	

Certain plants listed above will also
thrive in an adjacent temperature range.
These plants are indicated by symbols:
▲ = MILD   ■ = MODERATE

• Light pp.150–153
• Humidity pp.156–157
• Checklists pp.212–217

Plants lose water through their leaves in transpiration. The amount of water lost increases as the air gets drier and warmer. The moisture in the air is referred to as humidity. Since there is a limit to the amount of moisture the air can absorb, less water is given off by plants in highly humid conditions.

Plants from hot, dry regions need little humidity; indeed, they may suffer if the air around them is too humid. But many popular houseplants, such as large-leaved philodendrons, originated in rain forests and need a humid atmosphere to flourish.

Unless measures are taken to improve the level of humidity, the air in most modern homes will be too dry for many plants. Purpose-built humidifiers will do the job, but need to be supplemented by misting or strategic grouping of plants.

MISTING
Fine droplets of water sprayed on to a plant's leaves increase the local humidity and also deter red spider mites. Mist at any time of day in summer, but only do it in the morning in winter.

Large-leaved plants, such as painter's palette, especially benefit from misting. Hold a piece of card in front of the flower while misting around it. This will shield it from the damaging droplets of water.

PEBBLE TRAYS
Stand a group of plants in a tray filled with 2.5–5 cm of wet pebbles or gravel. Keep the level of the water below the bottom of the pots; but make sure the pebbles are constantly wet. Water that evaporates from the leaves as well as the tray will increase the local humidity around the group of plants.

GROUPING

Plants grown in small groups create a humid microclimate from which they all benefit. The plants' proximity to one another has the effect of reducing the circulation of air within the group. This means that the water evaporating from the plants during transpiration remains in the immediate atmosphere. However, there is a danger that if the air circulation is reduced too much, diseases such as grey mould may be encouraged.

SIGNS OF TOO DRY AN ATMOSPHERE

● Leaves wilt and fall off, especially from plants which are moisture lovers.
● Leaf tips turn brown, then shrivel, especially on plants with thin leaves, such as the peacock plant.
● Leaf edges turn yellow.
● The whole plant wilts if the temperature is high.
● Flowers fade prematurely and flower buds shrivel and fall off.
● Shoot tips wilt and shrivel.
● Leaves look dull and lacklustre.

SIGNS OF TOO HUMID AN ATMOSPHERE

● Plants with soft, furry or hairy leaves quickly decay.
● Flower petals and buds decay. They may even become covered with grey mould.
● Leaves decay, especially if moisture has become trapped at the point where leaves join the stem. They may also develop grey mould.
● Plants with tightly packed leaves or flowers will be the first to show signs of deterioration, especially when there is poor air circulation.
● Cacti and succulents develop patches of rot.

DOUBLE POTTING

Place a group of plants, each with its own pot, in a large container and pack moist peat around them. This increases the local humidity, isolates the compost in each pot from sudden temperature changes and keeps the compost moist for longer.

● Warmth pp.154–155

More houseplants die from too much water than from any other cause. Growing plants need a constant supply of water, but not so much that the compost becomes waterlogged. When this happens, the plant's roots cannot obtain the vital oxygen they need to perform their function of taking up water and minerals. As a result, leaves curl at their tips, flowers turn mouldy and roots rot. Underwatering can also be fatal, causing leaves to wilt and flowers to fall.

Plants need water to remain firm and upright. Mineral nutrients can only be absorbed and used by a plant if they are first dissolved in water. They may then be taken in by the leaves, but are absorbed mainly by the roots.

As plants lose moisture through tiny pores in their leaves so more water is drawn up from the roots. The warmer and drier the air, the faster this process of transpiration takes place. Water is also essential for photosynthesis, the process by which leaves manufacture food in the form of carbohydrates.

THE EFFECTS OF OVERWATERING

This sorry-looking plant (a hot water plant) has succumbed to the effects of too much water. Learn to recognize the symptoms of overwatering so that you can take prompt action to dry out the rootball in order to save the plant.

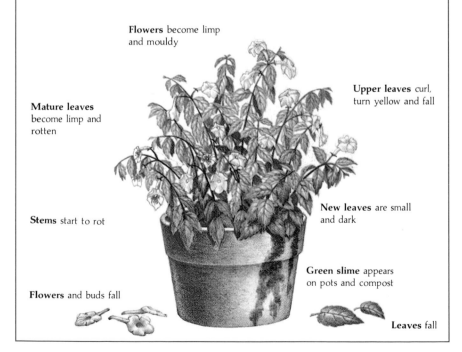

Flowers become limp and mouldy

Upper leaves curl, turn yellow and fall

Mature leaves become limp and rotten

New leaves are small and dark

Stems start to rot

Green slime appears on pots and compost

Flowers and buds fall

Leaves fall

REVIVING A WILTED PLANT

Drooping plants with wilted and falling leaves are probably parched. This may be due to your failure to water them at all or to ineffectual watering. For example, the compost may be so compacted that water cannot penetrate to the roots. Or a dried-out rootball may have contracted, leaving a gap at the side of the pot through which water simply runs straight out. In any event, take immediate steps to revive them.

Plants suffering from a lack of water have drooping leaves, stems and flower stalks.

Water will penetrate hard, dry compost more easily if you first break up the surface with a fork. Take care not to damage the roots.

Submerge the pot in a bucketful of water until bubbles stop rising from the compost. Mist the leaves. Allow excess water to drain away.

WHEN WATERING, REMEMBER.

● Whenever possible, water plants from below.
● Water plants in the morning if you can.
● Use tepid, not cold water.
● The larger the leaf area, the more water the plant needs.
● Plants need less water in winter because there is less light, the temperature is lower and the plant's metabolism is slower. But remember central heating dries out the air, so prevent plants from becoming parched in winter by misting when necessary.
● Plants in flower need constant moisture, even if they bloom in winter.
● Large plants in small pots need more water than large plants in large pots.
● Small plants in large pots need less water than small plants in small pots.
● Plants in unglazed clay pots need more water than plants in plastic pots.
● Plants grown in compost with sand and/or vermiculite added for drainage need more frequent watering than those planted in standard potting compost.
● Do not splash water on flowers or on to furry or hairy leaves.
● Do not pour water into the centre of any plant except into the urns of bromeliads.
● Do not splash water on leaves in strong sunlight. The droplets act like lenses and burn the leaves.
● Waterlogging, combined with cold, can be fatal.

● Watering/2 pp.160–161
● Feeding pp.162–163

Knowing when to water your plants and how much water to give them is probably the most important indoor gardening skill you can acquire. Each plant species, even different varieties of the same species, have different watering needs. Some need plenty of water all the time; others like moderate watering but only if their compost is allowed to dry out first; still other plants demand little water with periods of drought in between.

Get to know your plants by examining them regularly — weekly in cold, wet weather, and daily when it is hot and dry. Poke a pencil into the compost — if it comes out dry, the plant needs watering. Take care when doing this because you may easily damage the roots.

Dry compost weighs less and is lighter in colour than wet compost; it is also powdery and crumbly. Be on the alert for symptoms that indicate a plant is suffering from too dry a compost: foliage wilts, turns yellow and develops brown edges — it may even become dry and brittle to touch; flowers fade quickly and fall off prematurely.

The care instructions that come with many plants are prepared by experts and may suggest you water them sparingly, moderately or plentifully. They may also warn you that the plant has sensitive leaves. The illustrations on the right explain what these terms mean.

Water sparingly:
Let two-thirds of the compost dry out between each watering. Probe with a pencil to test for moisture. If dry, pour a little water on the surface and wait for it to seep down. No water should emerge from the base.

Water moderately:
Let the top 2 cm dry out between soakings. Probe with a pencil to test for moisture. Water the surface gently until a few drops emerge from the base. If watering from below, add a little at a time until it is absorbed.

Water plentifully:
Keep the compost damp at all times. Test with your fingertip. If dry, flood the pot to the rim until water flows from the base. Or water from below by filling the saucer until no more is absorbed. Then drain the compost well.

Sensitive leaves:
Hairy or quilted leaves may develop disfiguring blotches if water is left on them. Water a plant with these leaves from below. Stand it in a saucer of water and let it absorb what it wants.

SELF-WATERING CONTAINERS

For people who have little time to devote to plants, or are often away for short periods, self-watering containers can be a blessing. Water is automatically transferred from a reservoir to the compost in response to the plant's needs. Do not forget to check the water level regularly and top it up as required.

A **visual gauge** fitted to some self-watering containers indicates the water level in the reservoir.

HYDROCULTURE

You do not have to grow plants in compost. They can be grown in water alone, provided the water contains the right mineral nutrients. This method of growing plants is known as hydroculture or hydroponics.

A typical unit, illustrated below, consists of a large, water- and acid-proof container; a hydroponic plant pot; expanded clay granules to anchor the plant; a nutrient solution; water; a filling tube and water level indicator. Top the system up every 2–4 weeks. When the indicator shows minimum, do not add water straight away. Wait for 48 hours to allow air to reach the roots. Use tap water at room temperature and feed with special fertilizers according to instructions.

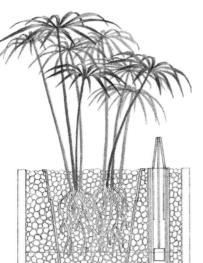

To convert a compost-grown plant to hydroculture, first wash off all compost from the roots by dunking them gently in a bowl of water.

Pack expanded clay granules round the roots and also fill the outer container. When the unit is assembled, add water.

Cover the plant with a clear, supported plastic bag. Keep it warm and shaded until established.

• Watering/1 pp.158–159
• Feeding pp.162–163
• Composts and Mixes pp.166–167

All plants need a balanced diet of mineral nutrients if they are to develop normally and grow strongly over a long period. For a houseplant, these nutrients are usually provided by the compost.

The mineral content of fresh compost is sufficient for a houseplant's needs, but once a plant has used them up, you need to add fertilizer to replace them. When dissolved in water and added to the compost these nutrients are taken up by the roots. Small amounts can also be absorbed by the leaves if you add fertilizer to the water you use for misting.

Nitrogen, phosphorus and potassium are the main mineral elements your houseplants need. They need other elements, too, such as iron and magnesium, but only in the minute amounts naturally present in all composts.

Nitrogen, supplied in the form of compounds called nitrates, is vital for the growth of stems and leaves. Because it is an important ingredient of the green pigment chlorophyll, nitrogen is needed to give leaves a good green colour.

Phosphorus, in the form of phosphates, is essential for healthy roots, for the development of flowers and the production of seeds and fruit. Potassium, in the form of potash, works in conjunction with nitrogen and phosphorus and balances their effects. By itself, it is essential for all-round, healthy growth.

A proprietary plant food will provide a balanced mineral supply for all houseplants. You can buy this food in the form of liquids, soluble powders, sticks and pills. Liquids and soluble powders are the best means of feeding your plants because they are easy to apply and reach all parts of the compost.

SAFETY FIRST WITH FERTILIZERS

- Carefully read the instructions accompanying the fertilizer.
- Always follow the recommended dosage. Do not experiment. If in doubt, remember it is better to underfeed than overfeed.
- Always use the same watering container. But do not use your feeding container for weedkiller or other chemicals. A minute amount of weedkiller can kill your plants.
- Dissolve the fertilizer in clean, fresh, tepid water.
- Do not mix more fertilizer than you will need in one day.
- Store fertilizers in a cool place and keep them away from children and animals.

LIQUIDS AND SOLUBLE POWDERS

These are the most common forms of fertilizers. They allow you to combine the watering and feeding tasks into one operation.

- Add the fertilizer to water, as directed on the container. Make sure the powder is dissolved.
- Make up enough to feed all your plants once. Do not keep a solution from one day to the next.
- Pour the solution directly on to the compost (see below).
- Spray a weak solution, known as a foliar feed, on to the foliage of tired-looking plants to revitalize them.
- Water plants before feeding if their compost is exceptionally dry.

When applying sticks and pills you need to use more care. You can physically damage the roots when pushing a stick or pill into the compost; and once they are implanted they give a strong local concentration of fertilizer which can damage the nearby roots. Slow-release products are on the market, but these have the disadvantage of releasing food long after a plant has entered its dormant period.

Feed your houseplants regularly while they are growing actively, developing new leaves and flowering. Except for winter-flowering plants, this active growth period usually lasts from early spring to the end of summer. For details of feeding individual plants, see the Plants in Profile section on pp.32–145.

Mix up a weak solution of fertilizer in a container with a long spout. Pour the solution over the whole surface of the compost.

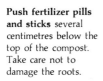

Push fertilizer pills and sticks several centimetres below the top of the compost. Take care not to damage the roots.

WHEN FEEDING, REMEMBER . . .
● Do not feed your houseplants when they are in their dormant period. Only feed them when they are actively growing.
● Do not feed plants immediately after they have been repotted in fresh compost. They should have enough food to last 6–8 weeks.
● Do not experiment with fertilizers. Follow the instructions recommended by the manufacturer.
● Overfeeding causes 'salt-burn' marks on leaves. These show up as brown spots on tips and scorched edges. Roots are also damaged by being 'burned'.
● Too much food in the compost shows up as a white deposit on the surface and on the outside of clay pots. To remedy this, water thoroughly once a week for several weeks to wash or leach out the excess food.
● Foliar feeds, given while misting, will revitalize plants, especially those with small root systems, such as bromeliads.
● Give a potash-rich feed on a single occasion after flowering plants have bloomed.
● Plants in sunny positions need feeding more often than plants in the shade.
● Loam-based composts have enough food for 6 months. Peat-based mixes have enough for only about 6 weeks.

● Composts and Mixes pp.166–167

The obvious and ideal way to make sure your houseplants survive your absence is to engage the services of a neighbour who knows how to treat plants and will not kill them with kindness.

Alternative measures can be more or less elaborate, depending on how long you will be away. A weekend's absence, except at the height of summer or in the depths of winter, presents few problems. Absences of up to a month demand effective means to ensure plants conserve water yet have access to fresh supplies.

WINTER VACATION GUIDELINES
These measures should be effective for up to 2 weeks. Before you leave, remember...
● Water each plant thoroughly, allowing excess to drain away.
● Move plants away from cold windowsills.
● Stand tender plants on top of the refrigerator where they can benefit from the warmth of its motor.
● Group plants on a plastic sheet in the centre of your warmest room. Or stand pots in a flat-bottomed tray containing about 18 mm of water.

SUMMER VACATION GUIDELINES
● For absences of 2–4 weeks, set up one or more self-watering systems (see right).
● For short absences of only a few days, water plants well and drain off the excess. Place them on a plastic sheet in the centre of a cool room and out of direct sunlight. A north- or east-facing room is usually best.

SELF-WATERING SYSTEMS
A number of methods that will satisfy your plants' water needs are fairly easy to set up. These include:
Capillary matting: This works best if the water reservoir is lower than the plants. A kitchen draining board (see right) is ideal. Use a blind to keep out the direct sun.
Wick-watering: For small groups of plants. Run a wick from a reservoir with a narrow neck into the top of the compost (see middle right). Keep water level in reservoir higher than the pot. Or insert wicks through the drainage holes of individual pots (see below right).
Tray reservoirs: Stand plants in a flat-bottomed tray with 18 mm water. Ask a neighbour to top up the reservoir during your absence.
Plastic bags: After a thorough watering, lower each small plant (but not ones with soft, furry leaves nor ones in flower) into a clear plastic bag. Tie the top tightly to keep moisture in and air out. For large plants, cover the pot and tie the bag around the plant's base (see below).

Soak a capillary mat in water and place it on the draining board. Rest one end in the sink containing several centimetres of water.

Place the plants on the mat – they will draw up what water they need without becoming waterlogged.

Insert a thick wick (available from hardware stores or garden centres) to

about 2.5 cm in the top of the compost. Trail the other end in a reservoir of water.

Remove the plant from its pot. Push a thick wick through the drainage hole and spread out its strands across the bottom of the pot. Cover with sand and replace the plant. Keep 5 cm of wick immersed in the reservoir and stand the pot clear of the water.

BEFORE YOU LEAVE . . .

● Check your plants for diseases or pests a week before you are due to leave. Isolate any plants that are not completely healthy.

● Group plants, if possible, in one area. They will all benefit from the proximity. Watering systems will be easier to set up and maintain in one area.

● Remove all fading flowers and their stalks, as they will be dead by the time you return and may cause healthy flowers to rot. Ask your plant-sitter, if you have organized one, to remove flowers as they fade and to pick up all leaves that fall off.

● Plants with large leaves, or a large number of small leaves, will need more water than those with few leaves.

● Ask your plant-sitter to rotate plants regularly to ensure all parts receive adequate amounts of light and their growth is balanced. Also ask them to check the level of water in any of your self-watering systems. Ask them to top these up if necessary.

● Close the door to the room where your plants are left to reduce draughts and to prevent the cat (if you have one) disturbing them.

● Humidity pp.156–157
● Watering pp.158–161

Compost provides a plant with mineral nutrients and moisture essential for its healthy growth. Soil taken directly from the garden is unsuitable for houseplants: confined to a container, it is unlikely to drain well; it also harbours pests, diseases and weed seeds.

Ready-made potting composts are available from garden centres. Based either on loam or peat, these are enriched with fertilizer and contain material for better drainage. The best known loam-based composts are the John Innes formulations recommended throughout this book (see below right).

Most plants thrive in one or other of these multi-purpose mixes, so long as they are given fertilizer at regular intervals. Plants such as ferns, cacti, succulents and orchids often do better in the mixes specially formulated for them.

Houseplants generally prefer an acid compost. Acidity and alkalinity are measured on what is called the pH scale. This scale ranges from 0, or extreme acidity, to 14, or extreme alkalinity. The middle of the scale, 7, is the point of neutrality. You can buy litmus paper from your local garden centre and test for yourself the acidity or alkalinity of a compost. Make a solution of compost and dip the litmus paper into it. If it turns red, the solution is acid; if it turns blue, the solution is alkaline. The pH of a ready-made compost is usually stated clearly on the package or bag.

The loam-based and peat-based composts are slightly acid and have a pH between 6 and 7. Composts with too much lime or chalk in them are alkaline, with a pH above 7. They upset a plant's metabolism and cause chlorosis in which leaves turn yellow before they die.

LOAM-BASED COMPOSTS

These are created by mixing partially sterilized loam (good quality soil), coarse sand and peat, with added plant foods.

Advantages and disadvantages:
- Most houseplants prefer loam-based to peat-based composts.
- Their effectiveness is reduced if the balance of the mixture is incorrect or the loam has not been properly sterilized. Always buy compost from a reputable retailer.
- Their weight provides a firm base for large plants.
- They are unlikely to dry out as rapidly or as completely as peat-based composts.
- They provide a better reservoir of trace elements for the plants' diet than peat-based types.

JOHN INNES COMPOSTS

First formulated in the 1930s, these composts are designed to satisfy the needs of most plants at their various stages of development. They include a seed compost and potting composts Nos. 1, 2 and 3. All potting composts contain the same amount of loam, coarse sand and peat, but No. 2 contains twice as much plant food as No. 1, and No. 3 contains three times as much. Most houseplants grow well at first in No. 1, and then, as they mature, are repotted into No. 2. Mixture No. 3 is only for mature plants in large pots.

• Feeding pp.162–163

PEAT-BASED COMPOSTS

These are called 'soilless' composts and are made from peat with plant foods and, possibly, coarse sand.

Advantages and disadvantages:

• They are easy to standardize so that one bag of compost is exactly the same as another of the same make. This can be important, as plants often suffer from a change in the quality of their compost at repotting time.

• They are better for small rather than large plants as they do not provide a firm base.

• Their food is used up rapidly and, as a result, fertilizer must be added frequently.

• They are preferred by some plants, such as African violets.

• They dry out rapidly and are difficult to moisten when very dry.

• They are more difficult to maintain at a uniform moisture content than are loam-based mixes.

• They are clean, light and easy to handle.

• They can be stored easily by sealing the bag and keeping it in a cool, dry place.

HOME-MADE COMPOSTS

Make up your own loam-based compost by mixing 1 or 2 parts of sterilized soil to 1 part of peat moss and 1 part coarse (sharp) sand.

Sterilize your garden soil by baking it in a covered container at 93°C (200°F) until the soil remains in the temperature range of 66–82°C (150–180°F) for half an hour.

To every 5 litres of the mix, add 12 millilitres of ground limestone and 8 millilitres of a granular fertilizer.

SPECIAL COMPOSTS

Most houseplants will grow in multipurpose potting composts provided fertilizer is added at regular intervals. However, some plants need, or at least thrive better on, slightly or entirely different composts.

• Cacti and succulents need a compost with good drainage to prevent them rotting. This is provided by a mix containing 1 part coarse sand to 2 parts of either a peat-based or a loam-based compost.

• Orchids need a very porous mix, composed of equal parts peat, sphagnum moss and osmunda fibre (from the fibrous roots of the osmunda or royal fern). The fibre can be substituted with pieces of tree bark.

• Insect-eating plants need a compost of the same porosity as orchids.

• Bromeliads need a porous compost free from lime, as is provided by equal parts of peat and coarse leaf mould.

• Cacti and Succulents pp.184–185   • Bromeliads pp.190–191   • Orchids and Insect-eating Plants pp.192–193

In order to look good and thrive, your plants must have healthy roots. Your main concerns are to make sure the roots of plants have sufficient water, food and air. But they also need the right space in the right sized pot. And roots are delicate and do not like to be disturbed.

When roots outgrow their pot, the plant is potbound and needs repotting or potting on. But do not repot just for the sake of it. Check to see if the roots are appearing through the drainage holes. Or gently remove the rootball from the pot —

if roots permeate the whole compost, the plant needs repotting. If not, replace it in its pot. Another sign that a plant needs repotting is top-heaviness.

Repot plants in spring so that the roots have a growing season to become established in their new quarters. Choose a pot that is slightly larger than the previous one and try to use the same type of compost (see p.171). Pots are usually clay or plastic — both have their advantages and disadvantages (see right).

The height of a pot is roughly the same

HANGING BASKETS

When setting up a hanging basket, remember it will become very heavy after watering. Screw a strong hook firmly into a joist, not into the ceiling plaster alone, and hang the basket on a chain or rope. Make the basket waterproof and use a drip-tray to prevent water ruining your floor or carpet.

A wire basket should only be used in a room with a water-resistant floor. Line the basket with a thick layer of damp sphagnum moss or a piece of plastic which has been cut to fit.

Show off your trailing plants to best advantage in an attractive container suspended on macramé ropes. But if your container has no drainage holes, make sure you put a layer of crocks at the bottom.

Make a few holes in the bottom of the plastic for the water to drain away. Cover the plastic with a thick layer of moist, loam-based compost.

Indoor hanging baskets with built-in drip-trays to catch excess water can be used in carpeted rooms. Remember to water in moderation — do not flood the drip-tray to overflowing.

Position your plant on top of the compost. Trickle in more compost to fill the basket to within 2.5 cm of the rim. Drape the trailing stems over the side, water the compost thoroughly and drain.

as its diameter. Half-pots on the other hand have the same diameter range as ordinary pots, but not the depth. They are useful for bromeliads, which need little compost as their roots are for anchorage mainly, and cacti, which do not have an extensive run of roots. Other plants that will thrive in half-pots include painted net leaf and tradescantia.

Wooden or plastic tubs can be used for plants that have become too large for the range of ordinary pots. The wooden tubs are often old barrels which have been cut in half. If you have to make drainage holes for yourself, use a drill about 12 mm in diameter and space the holes evenly across the bottom of the tub.

The sizes of pots
A pot is classified by the diameter across the inside of the rim. Its depth is normally about the same size. Pots are made in a range of sizes from 4 cm to 38 cm. Usually only 5 sizes are used (*right*). 25 cm or even 38 cm pots may be used for very large floor-standing plants.

6 cm

8 cm

13 cm

18 cm

25 cm

CLAY OR PLASTIC POTS?
- Clay pots are heavier to handle.
- Plastic pots do not usually break if dropped.
- Both types need to be stored under cover in winter. Porous clay pots are damaged by frost and ice. Some plastic pots become brittle and fracture at low temperatures.
- Clay pots are harder to clean than plastic ones.
- Clay pots have a natural colour that blends well with most plants.
- The porous nature of clay pots allows salts that might damage plants, but also minerals that are beneficial, to escape.
- Clay pots need to be soaked in clean water a day before they are used, otherwise they will take moisture from the compost.
- Clay pots provide a heavier base for large plants. Plastic pots, especially when filled with a peat-based compost, are easily capsized.
- Plants in clay pots need more frequent watering because excess water evaporates through the sides and dries out the compost. Because of this, plants in clay pots are less likely to become waterlogged.
- The compost in clay pots remains cooler in summer and warmer in winter.
- Plastic pots are lightweight and easier to handle.
- Plastic pots are better for use in self-watering systems, especially capillary matting.
- Plastic pots are available in a wider range of colours.

• Compost and Mixes
pp.166–167

TOPDRESSING

If you do not wish to move plants on to larger-sized pots, either because you want to curtail their growth or because they are already in the largest size you want, you can revitalize them every spring by top-dressing (see right). Plants such as hippeastrums, which usually thrive on being potbound and dislike having their roots disturbed, may also be topdressed.

For plants that cannot be repotted yet do not respond to topdressing, root pruning is an alternative, albeit a drastic one because your plant may not survive. Remove the rootball from the pot and, with a sharp knife, cut slices 2.5 cm thick from the sides and base. Replace the plant in its old pot and fill the newly-created space with fresh compost.

REPOTTING

Most plants should be repotted, or potted on, when their roots fill their pots. This can be every year for fast-growing plants. However, never repot until it is necessary.

The time for repotting arrives when you notice roots emerging through the drainage holes or the compost drying out rapidly. A top-heavy plant, or one obviously too large for its pot, are further signs that repotting is needed.

Removing large plants from their pots to see if they are potbound (see right) can be a tricky business and you may need some help. If the roots have grown through the holes and taken a hold on the pot, you may have to cut them away from the rootball with a sharp knife or scalpel. If the pot is clay, you may have to break it.

With a spoon, remove the top 2.5–5 cm of old compost from around the plant. Make sure you do not damage the roots. Refill the pot with fresh compost of the same type as the original and firm it down around the plant's stem.

To remove a large plant from its pot, first lay the pot on its side. Holding the plant gently but firmly, rotate the pot slowly and tap its rim with a small wooden block.

Run a knife blade around between the rootball and the pot. Ask a friend to hold the pot while you ease the plant out.

STEP BY STEP REPOTTING

Before removing the plant from its old pot, have the new one ready. It should be clean and a size larger. For plants in 6 cm pots, use an 8 cm one; for plants in 8 cm pots, use a 13 cm one, and so on.

Soak all unglazed clay pots in clean water overnight and allow to dry for an hour. This will prevent the pot from absorbing all the moisture from the fresh compost. Water the plant a couple of hours prior to repotting and let it drain.

Place a 12–18 mm layer of crocks in the bottom of the pot. Remove the plant from its pot by supporting the upturned rootball with one hand and knocking the pot's rim on a firm surface (see right). Remove the old crocks from the base of the rootball and tease out matted roots.

Cover the crocks in the new pot with a 12 mm layer of peat plus a thick layer of potting mix. Place the rootball in the pot so that its top is between 12 mm and 4 cm below the rim, depending on the pot's size.

For big plants, leave a 4 cm space at the top of the compost for watering. For small plants, leave a 12 mm space; for plants in 25 cm pots, leave a depth of 2.5–4 cm.

Spread the roots out and trickle in compost around the plant, filling the pot to the desired level. Tap the pot several times to settle the compost, then firm it around the plant.

An alternative method of repotting involves preparing a 'mould' of fresh compost inside the new, larger pot. Place the old pot, after removing the plant, on to a layer of compost inside the new pot and fill the space between the pots with compost. Then place the rootball of the plant into the 'mould' and firm the mixture around the stem.

To remove a small plant from its pot, first put your hand on the top of the pot, with two fingers either side of the plant's stem.

Turn the pot upside down and gently knock its rim against a firm surface, rotating the pot as you do so. The rootball should easily come away in your hand.

Before you repot the plant, place a layer of crocks over the drainage holes. Cover the crocks with a layer of peat and compost to bring the rootball to the desired level in the pot.

Put the rootball in the middle of the new pot and fill the space around it with compost. Firm it down around the stem and thoroughly soak from above to settle it. Allow the excess to drain.

• Composts and Mixes
pp.166–167

Your plants will not look their best unless you groom them regularly and judiciously. They will continue to grow and change in response to the conditions around them, not in straight lines or in shapes that always please the eye.

Flowers fade and fall, lower leaves turn yellow and brown, stems grow leggy or creep without restraint. And plants are sensitive, living things that get knocked, bruised, chilled, overwatered or scorched by the sun. You cannot expect them to look good all the time.

It is up to you to prune your plants occasionally to control their shape, to train climbing stems or to trim them to keep them neat. Pick off dead or fading flowers and remove leaves that are broken or have lost their colour. And remember that regular cleaning of leaves to remove dust and dirt will improve the looks and health of your plants.

STAKING AND SUPPORTING

Climbing plants grown indoors need some form of support such as a pole, trellis or wire. It should be sturdy, functional and unobtrusive – unless you want to make a feature of it.

Put supports in place before your plant needs staking to allow shoots to grow up, through or around them. If necessary, tie a shoot to a support with soft, green string and loop the string under a leaf-joint.

Hoops of split cane or wire offer alternative and attractive ways to train some plants such as pink jasmine and wax flowers (see pp.200–201). Provide a moss-covered pole for plants with aerial roots (see below).

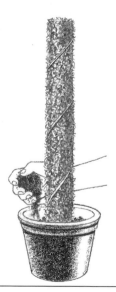

A moss-covered pole is the best way to support a Swiss cheese plant or a philodendron. Wrap a layer of sphagnum moss, 5–7.5 cm thick, around a wooden stake which is tall enough to allow for fairly rapid growth. As you wrap the moss, bind it criss-cross fashion to the stake with plastic-covered wire. Fix the pole to the bottom of the pot with Plaster of Paris and fill the pot with compost.

Position the plant in the pot and help the stem and aerial roots to spiral their way up the pole. Initially, they may need to be tied with string until they get a hold. Make sure you mist the pole at least once a day in summer to keep the roots soft and to maintain a humid atmosphere.

• Plants in Profile
  pp.101, 105

LOOKING AFTER LEAVES

Dust and dirt, particularly in industrial areas and inner cities, can be detrimental to your plants. They prevent light reaching the cells where photosynthesis takes place. They also clog up the tiny pores on the leaves, hindering the movement of oxygen, carbon dioxide and water into and out of the leaves. This movement is essential for the processes of respiration, transpiration and photosynthesis.

You should remove the dust and dirt regularly by cleaning the leaves with a soft, damp cloth. Proprietary leaf-shining fluids are available but they are not recommended as they, too, may clog the pores and damage the leaves. Milk, beer, vinegar and olive oil are often suggested as substitutes, but clean water is best. If you need to use a little soap, make sure you rinse it away with fresh water.

Remember that water or any other fluids will damage hairy or quilted leaves. Instead, use a soft, dry brush to clean plants with these leaves.

When cleaning leaves, do not press heavily on them. Support the leaf with one hand and wipe gently with the other. Remember that you should never clean leaves while the plant is in strong or direct sunlight. And always clean leaves in the morning, especially in winter, to allow them to dry out before nightfall. Leaves that remain cold and damp overnight will attract disease.

Waxy, shiny or glossy leaves should be lightly dusted before being wiped with a clean, damp sponge or cloth. This avoids unattractive, dusty smears when they dry.

Hairy or quilted leaves, as well as cacti and succulents, should not be washed but dusted with a soft, dry brush.

Small plants, or plants with many small leaves, can be washed by immersing them in a bucket of tepid water. Remember to hold the plant's stem to stop it falling out of the pot.

LOOKING AFTER STEMS

Houseplants can become too large or unbalanced if you fail to keep them tidy. When their stems grow too long or straggly, you will have to prune them back or pinch out their growing tips. Pruning encourages the growth of new, previously dormant shoots close to the area of the cut.

Spring is the best time to cut back stems, especially those of trailing and climbing plants and of stems that have lost all their leaves. This will give the cut-back stems the whole growing season to establish themselves.

Use a sharp knife or scissors to prune soft stems. Make the cut at a slight angle just above a leaf joint. Use secateurs for semi-hard and hard stems and make the cut just above a growth bud.

To encourage a plant to become bushy and to fill out with leaves, pinch out the soft, growing tips with your thumb and forefinger. This is called 'stopping' or 'nipping' and is important for tradescantias, zebrinas and other trailing plants. The stem must be growing and must have at least three leaves. The plant will respond by sending out new sideshoots from dormant buds along the stem. At a later date, you can pinch out the growing tips of these sideshoots to produce even thicker growth.

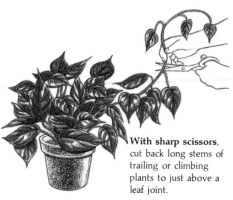

With sharp scissors, cut back long stems of trailing or climbing plants to just above a leaf joint.

Pinching out the growing tips of straggly stems redirects the energies of a plant and encourages the growth of sideshoots.

The plant becomes bushier as new sideshoots grow – pinch some of these out in turn to maintain bushiness.

Snip off the brown tips of leaves with sharp scissors. Make the cut in the green, healthy part of the leaf. Sometimes it is better to remove the leaf completely.

IMPROVING FLOWERS

Dead or fading flowers are both unsightly and a drain on a plant's resources. Pinch them out or cut them off with scissors. This keeps the plant looking tidy and encourages further flower buds to open. It also means that the plant will not waste its energy on producing seeds. Dead flowers, whether they are on the plant or have fallen beside it, attract disease – so remove them daily.

When removing faded and dead flowers from cyclamen, also remove the stem. Do this by twisting and pulling it gently. Leaving bare stems attached to the plant is unsightly and encourages disease.

TOOLS YOU WILL NEED

- Sharp scissors are essential for pruning, trimming and cutting back soft shoots and stems. Use secateurs for hard stems. Knives must be very sharp and used with dexterity – take care not to injure yourself.
- Green string is indispensable for tying stems to supports, especially for climbers. Use plastic-covered wire to bind moss to the wooden stake when making a moss pole.
- Wooden stakes and wire loops are useful for supporting climbers.
- A sponge and a soft brush are needed for cleaning leaves.

WHEN GROOMING PLANTS, REMEMBER . . .

- If you use soapy water to clean leaves, use as little soap as possible and rinse the leaves thoroughly afterward.
- When cleaning the leaves of flowering plants make sure you do not splash water drops on to the blooms.
- After cleaning a plant, make sure all traces of water are removed. Check the leaves, joints and any 'corner' that may trap water.
- Clear up dead flowers and leaves that have fallen from plants or they will attract disease.
- Do not use a blunt knife or a pair of loose-bladed scissors to remove dead flowers and leaves. These will tear and bruise the plant's tissue, so allowing access for disease.
- Do not cut off aerial roots from climbing plants. Mist them instead to keep them soft.
- Cut off all-green shoots from variegated plants – they grow more quickly than variegated shoots and soon dominate the plant.
- When tying the stems of climbing plants to a support, make sure you give the stems plenty of room to grow. If they are tied tightly, stems of flowering plants will produce blooms that are squashed together. Stems that are congested have poor air circulation and attract mildew.

• Plants in Profile pp.68, 126–127

Raising your own houseplants can be simple, rewarding and inexpensive. Your established plants may have grown unattractive, or you may wish to propagate particular favourites. The most common method is known as vegetative propagation. This means taking cuttings from stems or leaves; dividing stems; air-layering a stem; or potting up offsets. You can also grow certain foliage and most flowering houseplants from seeds.

SOFT-STEM CUTTINGS

Many soft-stemmed plants can be propagated in spring from the top of a healthy stem or shoot. With a sharp knife, cut between 7.5 and 13 cm of stem (the thicker the stem, the longer the cutting) just below a leaf-joint. Dip its end into hormone rooting powder. Insert it to a third of its length in equal parts moist peat and sharp sand. Firm the mix around it and lightly water it. Keep it warm and water when necessary. Once it has rooted, pot it up in John Innes potting compost No. 1.

A tip cutting should have at least three leaf nodes between the tip and the base. Remove unwanted leaves at the base.

SEMI-HARD STEM OR 'HEEL' CUTTINGS

Plants with semi-hard stems, such as hibiscus, can be increased from a sideshoot pulled away from the main stem. This cutting should be from a non-flowering shoot; if this is not possible, remove flowers and buds.

Remove the sideshoot by tugging it firmly downward, making sure you take with it a 'heel' or small piece of the main stem. With a knife, cut away lower leaves. Do not pull them off.

Cleanly cut off all the loose ends on the 'heel' — damaged tissue will rot, leading to a spread of decay upward into the cutting. Moisten the heel, dip it into hormone rooting powder and insert it into a pot containing equal parts moist peat and sharp sand. Firm the mix around the cutting, water lightly and cover with a plastic bag to retain moisture. Once it has rooted, pot it up in John Innes potting compost No. 1.

Hold the main stem firmly and tug the sideshoot downward. Take with it a 'heel' or small piece of main stem, if possible with some bark still attached.

Trim off any loose ends around the heel with a sharp knife. Be careful not to damage the tissue of the cutting or it may rot.

SEEDS

To germinate, seeds need moisture, air and a temperature between 18–24°C (64–75°F). Most prefer darkness, although a few, such as primulas, do better in light.

Fill a seed tray to within 12 mm of the rim with John Innes seed compost or a peat-based mix. Sprinkle seeds thinly and evenly and cover them with fine compost to about four times their own thickness. Water compost gently but well, cover the tray with a sheet of glass and newspaper, and leave the tray in a warm place.

After the seeds have germinated, remove the glass. When large enough to handle, lift the seedlings with a light instrument such as a plant marker, holding them gently by a seed leaf. Pot them up individually into pots containing John Innes potting compost No. 1.

Keep seeds warm and dark until they germinate. Remember to turn the glass daily to prevent problems caused by condensation.

LEAF-STEM (LEAF-PETIOLE) CUTTINGS

Some fleshy-leaved plants can be propagated from a leaf and its stalk. With a knife, cut a healthy, mature leaf close to the main stem. Either insert it into a mixture (see below) or let it root in water. Fix a plastic cover over a glass of water with a rubber band. Pierce a hole and insert the cutting so 2 cm of stalk is below water. Keep the water topped up. When roots are 2.5 cm long, pot up in John Innes potting compost No. 1.

Cut off a healthy, mature leaf with a sharp knife. Trim the stalk to about 4 cm (*below*) and dip into hormone rooting powder.

Fill and firm a pot with moist peat and sharp sand. Make a hole 2.5 cm deep and insert the cutting.

To retain moisture, cover the pot with a clear plastic bag kept away from the cutting by split canes.

When a new plantlet has grown, pot up in John Innes potting compost No. 1.

• Compost and Mixes pp.166–167   • Pots and Repotting pp.168–171

LEAVES WITHOUT STALKS

Large-leaved begonias can grow new plants from leaves without stalks, or even from pieces of leaf (see right). Cut a healthy, mature leaf, turn it upside down and make a few small slits in the prominent veins with a sharp knife.

Fill a large pot with equal parts moist peat and sharp sand. Place the leaf, cut-side down, in contact with the mixture and peg it there with bent pieces of wire. Cover the pot with clear plastic. In 2–3 weeks, plantlets will grow from the slit veins. Separate them with a knife and pot them up into John Innes potting compost No. 1.

CUTTINGS FROM LEAF PIECES

An alternative way of propagating large-leaved begonias is to cut up a single leaf into a number of pieces. This can also be done with the non-variegated sansevierias.

With a sharp knife, cut a healthy, mature leaf into squares (begonias) or strips across the entire leaf (sansevierias). Snip the lower edges to indicate which is the stalk end. Insert the pieces, stalk-end down, to a depth of 12–18 mm in equal parts moist peat and sharp sand. Firm the mixture around the base of the cuttings and cover the pot with clear plastic. When shoots have grown from the base of the cuttings, pot them up into John Innes potting compost No. 1.

Choose a healthy, mature begonia leaf and cut off the stalk close to the leaf. Then cut half a dozen small slits in the large veins where they branch into smaller ones.

Remove the plant from the pot and, holding the rootball in one hand, detach a healthy, mature leaf with the other.

Cut sansevieria leaves into strips using a sharp knife. Cut begonia leaves into squares.

Peg the leaf firmly and cut-side down on to the mixture.

When young plantlets have reached 2.5 cm across, remove and pot them up individually.

Insert the leaf pieces vertically and stalk-end down into the mixture.

DIVISION

Plants with clumps of fibrous roots and several shoots can be increased easily and quickly by dividing them in spring. These include spider plants and prayer plants.

Hold the plant firmly and remove the rootball from the pot. Find a place in the clump where the plant can be divided and, with your fingers, gently ease the stems apart.

If you have to disentangle roots, try to keep as much of the original compost as possible to avoid damaging the tiny root hairs. You may also need a sharp knife to begin the process of division, but be careful not to damage the roots.

Pot up each separated clump into John Innes potting compost No. 1. Cover the base of a pot with crocks and a layer of compost. Holding the clump in one hand, trickle compost around it to fill the pot.

OFFSETS

Offsets and offshoots are replicas of their parents that grow from the base of certain plants. These include succulents, such as some aloes; bromeliads, such as aechmeas and vrieseas; and sansevierias.

In spring, remove the plant from its pot and, using a sharp knife, detach a good-sized offset from its parent. Remember to cut as close to the parent as possible and to take some roots with it.

Insert the offset into equal parts moist peat and sharp sand to the same depth as it was on the parent. Keep the mixture moist but not too wet. Position the pot in medium light at a temperature between 18—24°C (64—75°F). When roots have formed, pot up the offset into John Innes potting compost No. 1.

Find a suitable spot at which to prise the shoots apart. Try to retain as much of the original compost as possible.

Pot up the separated clumps in pots just bigger than the spread of the roots. Firm the compost around the plant, water well and keep shaded until established.

Cut the offset close to the main stem, taking roots with it if there are some.

When the root system is established, pot up and treat as a mature plant.

• Compost and Mixes
pp.166—167

• Pots and Repotting
pp.166—171

AIR-LAYERING

This method is used primarily for plants with thick, sturdy stems, such as rubber plants, Swiss cheese plants and dracaenas, that have outgrown themselves or the space you can provide for them. Air-layering also gives a new lease of life to plants that look less attractive having lost most of their lower leaves.

Air-layering is a means of cutting a plant down to the size you want by encouraging new roots to grow at a chosen point on the stem, close to the lowest healthy leaf. The method is described on the right. When the new plant is cut off, the original stem can be cut back to a suitable length and encouraged to grow anew. The original stem of a dracaena can be cut into sections and used to grow more plants as described on p.181.

Make a cut slanting upward within 10 cm of the lowest healthy leaf. Dust the cut with hormone rooting powder and wedge it open with a matchstick.

Wrap an open-ended plastic bag around the cut and tie the bottom firmly with tape or strong thread. Pack moist peat or sphagnum moss into the bag until it covers the cut. Then tie the top of the plastic.

In about 6–8 weeks, new roots should be growing through the peat. Remove the plastic and, holding the stem firmly, sever it under the roots (*below*) and pot it up in John Innes potting compost No. 1.

Old plant   **New plant**

Give the new plant the support of a cane, if necessary, until it becomes established.

The original stem can be kept and encouraged to develop new shoots.

PLANTLETS

Some plants, such as the spider plant, mother of thousands and the piggy-back plant, produce plantlets, small replicas of themselves that can be potted up.

Spider plants produce plantlets on the ends of long runners. Peg a plantlet, still attached to the runner of its parent, into a pot containing equal parts moist peat and sharp sand. Alternatively, stand the parent in a tray (see below).

Piggy-back plants grow plantlets on mature leaves. Cut a leaf with a healthy plantlet and about 2.5 cm of stalk. Insert the stalk into a small pot containing moist peat and sharp sand. Make sure the part with the plantlet is in contact with the rooting mix. When new growth signals the formation of roots, transfer to a standard potting mix.

Peg the plantlets of a spider plant to the mix with bent pieces of wire. Keep moist, warm and in medium light until leaves are about 7.5 cm long. Then sever plantlets from their runners and pot up individually.

THICK STEM CUTTINGS

Plants with thick stems, such as yuccas, dumb canes and cordylines, can be propagated from pieces of stem in spring. Cut the stem into short sections and include at least one leaf node in each. Half bury the section horizontally in equal parts moist peat and sharp sand. When new growth from the node is well established, repot into John Innes potting compost No. 1.

Stem sections can be planted vertically. Make sure you plant each with the bottom end downward as it was on the original stem.

Cut the stem into sections, each 7.5 to 10 cm long. Make sure each has at least one leaf node. If the nodes are not clearly visible, they should be indicated by scarring or by lines encircling the stem.

When planting horizontally, half bury the sections.

Leaves will grow from upper nodes, roots from nodes buried in the mix.

• Compost and Mixes pp.166–167   • Pots and Repotting pp.168–171

Some of the most flamboyant of all flowering houseplants are grown from bulbs. These are fleshy, underground organs that store food during the plant's dormant period. When growing actively, they produce roots, leaves and flowers.

Plants with large bulbs, such as hyacinths, daffodils, hippeastrums and tulips, are often specially prepared so that they will flower out of season at Christmastime. This is called forcing because the bulbs can be forced into flower many weeks before they would naturally do so outdoors. Of these large bulbs, hyacinths are the easiest to force, while tulips are the hardest. Details of how to bring these bulbs into flower are given below, on the opposite page and in the Plants in Profile section.

Bulb fibre is the best medium in which to cultivate bulbs because it is clean, easy-to-handle and very porous. Loam-based or peat-based composts can also be used. But do not use bulb fibre for bulbs which you intend to plant outdoors after they have flowered.

PLANTING SPECIALLY-PREPARED BULBS

Choose bulbs of the same size and variety in order to get blooms of the same height flowering at the same time. They must be kept cool and dark to encourage roots to grow and then given warmth and light to bring on the leaves and flowers.

Moisten the bulb fibre or John Innes seed compost thoroughly before planting as many bulbs as the container will hold comfortably. If you use bulb fibre, the container does not need drainage holes.

Set the bulbs close together, neither touching each other nor the container. Press the compost firmly but not tightly around the bulbs leaving their noses exposed. Cover with newspaper or a black plastic bag.

Leave in a cool, dark place for about 6–10 weeks and keep moist. When shoots emerge, remove the bag or newspaper. When the shoots are 5 cm high, move to a cool, shady room. After 2 weeks, move to warmth and better light.

• Plants in Profile pp.34–35, 38–39, 42–43

PLANTS WITH SMALL BULBS

Crocuses, irises, snowdrops, grape hyacinths, scillas and other small bulbs cannot be successfully forced into flower at Christmas-time. However, they can be encouraged to flower indoors two weeks or so before they would naturally do so outdoors.

They should be planted in autumn in small, well-drained pots containing John Innes seed compost or bulb fibre. Plant several bulbs close together, but not touching, with their tops completely covered by the compost.

Store the pots in a cool place for eight to ten weeks and keep the compost moist. When shoots appear above the compost and flower buds are ready to open, move the plants to a cool, shady room. After a few days, encourage flowering by moving them to a brighter spot that is free from draughts and high temperatures. Remember to keep the compost moist at all times. After flowering, treat the plants in the same way as larger bulbs, such as hyacinths.

Hyacinth glass
Grow hyacinths hydroponically in a special bulb glass filled to the neck with water. Add 2 pieces of charcoal to keep the water sweet. Sit the bulb in the neck but above the water. Keep cool and shaded until shoots appear. Bring the glass into warmth and light and turn it regularly to keep the flower stem straight.

SUCCESS WITH FORCED BULBS

● Buy hyacinth, daffodil, tulip or hippeastrum bulbs which have been specially prepared if you want bulbs that flower out of season at Christmas-time.

● Only buy bulbs that are disease-free and firm.

● Plant in a well-drained bowl, otherwise the flowers will rot.

● Keep dark and cool to allow the roots to grow before the shoots. Cover the bowl with newspaper or a black plastic bag and keep in total darkness at 4.5°C (40°F). If it is kept too warm, the leaves become deformed and the plants stunted.

● Keep the compost moist, otherwise flowers will not form.

● Do not leave bulbs too long under cover otherwise the shoots will grow too tall, causing the leaves to become soft and limp.

● When shoots are 4–5 cm high, move the bowl to a cool, shaded room at 10°C (50°F). If it is any warmer, the flowers will not develop.

● After two weeks, move to a draughtless spot in better light, otherwise leaves turn yellow.

● After flowering, cut off dead flowers and feed plants every 10 days with a weak fertilizer until leaves wither.

● Remove withered leaves and keep bowl in a cool, dry place indoors. If you can plant bulbs outdoors, do so in late summer. They cannot be forced again indoors.

● Feeding pp.162–163   ● Composts and Mixes pp.166–167

All cacti are succulents, but not all succulents are cacti. This distinction between these two often causes confusion. Cacti belong to the same family and have woolly or bristly cushions called areoles from which grow spines, long hairs or short hooks. Once in the life of each areole, a flower grows. All succulents have fleshy leaves or stems which can store water. This enables them to survive dry periods when moisture is unavailable.

Of the two kinds of cacti, desert cacti are more numerous than forest cacti. They come from regions where there is plenty of sun and little moisture for long periods, and then a huge downpour of rain. Forest cacti, such as the Easter and Christmas cacti, come from the rain-forest regions of tropical America where, as epiphytes, they grow attached to trees. They need shade from the hottest sun, and water through most of the year.

MAKING A CACTUS GARDEN
Plant a miniature landscape of cacti and succulents in a bowl. Choose from a variety of shapes, sizes and colours, but select those that enjoy the same growing conditions. Living stones (*Lithops*) alongside real pebbles add an attractive and unusual dimension. Adequate drainage is provided by a container with holes or a layer of gravel 2.5 cm deep below the mix. This can be either cactus compost or 2 parts John Innes potting compost No. 1 and 1 part coarse sand. Water the mixture sparingly and keep the bowl in a sunny spot.

Jade tree, *Crassula argentea*: This succulent grows up to 1.2 m tall and has shiny, jade-green leaves shaped like a spoon. In winter, it produces tiny, pink or white flowers in clusters 5–7.5 cm across.

SUCCESS WITH DESERT CACTI
- Feed in summer to encourage flowering.
- Keep roots restricted to encourage flowering. Repot only when roots fill the pot.
- Provide winter nighttime temperatures of 10–13°C (50–55°F) even though they can survive lower. Exceptions include the old man cactus, *Cephalocereus senilis*, which needs 15°C (59°F).
- Full sun is essential. Provide light shade at noon on hot summer days.
- Keep compost moist in summer with tepid water. Keep barely moist in winter. Do not mist.

SUCCESS WITH FOREST CACTI
- Provide temperatures of 13–15°C (55–59°F) during dormant periods: February and March for Christmas cacti; October to early February for Easter cacti; late November to late February for epiphyllums.
- Provide slightly diffused light.
- Mist in summer and when not in flower.
- Keep compost moist. When dormant, keep compost barely moist.

Hedgehog cactus, *Echinocereus pectinatus*: This desert cactus grows 25 cm high and 7.5 cm wide. It has a stout, upright, medium green stem with vertical ribs smothered with white spines. The violet-pink flowers are 7.5 cm across.

SUCCESS WITH SUCCULENTS
- Provide winter nighttime temperatures of 10–13°C (50–55°F), although they can survive lower.
- Provide bright light, but light shade at noon on hot summer days.
- Water the compost regularly in summer when it dries. Keep barely moist in winter. Do not mist.
- Grow succulents in shallow pots, repotting only when potbound.

Goat's horn cactus, *Astrophytum capricorne*: This roughly spherical, deeply segmented, light green, desert cactus grows 25 cm high and 12.5 cm wide. It has white, woolly scales and brown, wavy spines. The flowers are many-petalled, 5 cm across and yellow with red centres.

• Feeding pp.162–163   • Composts and Mixes pp.166–167

Historically, ferns are among the oldest plants on earth. They were also among the earliest houseplants — with the cast iron plant and palms, they were extremely popular in the 19th century. They differ from nearly all other plants because they do not produce flowers and seeds. Instead they reproduce by means of spores.

Most ferns grown indoors come from tropical or subtropical regions. In the wild they may grow as epiphytes, anchored to the branches or trunks of trees, or on the forest floor in shady, humid places that are rich in leaf mould.

They usually grow from a fleshy, storage organ called a rhizome which is often covered in fur or scales. This covering is brown, black or silvery-white. Their fronds vary considerably in size and shape from the graceful, arched fronds of the ladder fern to the antler-like fronds of the stag's horn fern.

If you are to grow them successfully indoors, you will need to match as closely as possible the conditions in which they thrive in the wild. In general, whether they come from temperate or tropical regions, they are all moisture lovers. If you can also provide them with a temperature of 15°C (59°F) to 21°C (70°F), dappled light and fresh air, they will produce new fronds throughout the year.

Ladder fern
Nephrolepis exaltata

Hen and chicken fern
Asplenium bulbiferum

• Plants in Profile pp.64–65,
  136–137, 140–141

FERNS FOR BEGINNERS

The ladder fern, *Nephrolepis exaltata*, is easy to grow and looks impressive on a plant pedestal (see below left) where all its fronds can freely cascade.

The button fern, *Pellaea rotundifolia*, has unusual, deep green, button-like leaflets attached to long, wiry stems.

The hen and chicken fern, *Asplenium bulbiferum*, grows plantlets called bulbils on its fronds. These can be readily rooted to produce new plants (see below middle).

The bird's nest fern, *Asplenium nidus*, is more difficult to grow but as long as it has diffused light in summer, and warmth in winter, little can go wrong.

Stag's horn fern
Platycerium bifurcatum

An attractive and eye-catching way to grow a stag's horn fern is on a piece of tree bark. Wrap the root mass in coarse peat and sphagnum moss and tie it with strong cotton twine to the bark. Keep the roots and the bark continually moist until the roots have taken hold.

SUCCESS WITH FERNS

● Provide moderate temperatures of 10–15 °C (50–59 °F), but not lower than 7 °C (45 °F) for most ferns.

● Do not let the compost dry out. Even in winter, keep the roots damp. Water more freely in summer. Excess water can rot the roots, so provide good drainage.

● Moist air is essential, especially in summer. Mist the plants frequently with clean water. In winter, do this only in the morning to allow the fronds to dry before nightfall.

● Provide diffused, indirect light. Ferns are not lovers of deep shade but they do need to be kept out of direct sunlight in summer.

● Feed ferns in summer but do not give strong solutions of fertilizer as these will damage the roots and prevent them from taking up an adequate supply of water.

DISTRESS SIGNALS

● The tips and edges of fronds turn brown and brittle if the compost is too dry. Eventually the fronds will wither.

● Young fronds turn pale yellow if the air is too dry.

● Fronds turn pale and weak if the ferns are not fed regularly in summer.

● Brown scorch marks appear on the fronds if ferns are kept in strong sunlight.

● Fronds turn yellow at their bases if the air is too warm. Mature fronds will eventually turn brown and fall if this is not rectified.

● Feeding pp.162–163

The elegance and grace of palms have made them favourite plants for parlours and hotel foyers since the 19th century. Their crowns of fan-shaped or feathery fronds soften harsh angles and today bring a popular tropical flavour into the home.

In the wild, they flower and fruit, and may grow up to 30 m high. Indoors, they are smaller, longer-lasting and slower-growing, producing at best three fronds each year.

A palm's growth at first fills out the girth of its trunk. When this has reached its maximum size, the palm then starts to grow in height. Each stem of a palm has only one growing point, the terminal bud, from which all the fronds develop. If this is damaged, the palm will stop growing and eventually die.

Palms are fairly easy-going and do not need much attention. They thrive in a range of light conditions and temperatures so long as they are kept free from draughts and extremes of heat, and out of bright, direct sunlight. They appreciate a fairly humid atmosphere and a moist but not waterlogged compost.

European fan palm
Chamaerops humilis

Pygmy date palm
Phoenix roebelenii

• Plants in Profile pp.129, 132–133

PROBLEMS WITH PALMS

Brown leaf tips may be caused by a constantly dry atmosphere, draughts or a dry compost. In summer, dry air encourages red spider mites.

Yellow leaves result from a dry compost in summer. If it has become very dry, soak the compost thoroughly.

Lower leaves often turn brown with age. Do not tear them from the frond but cut them off close to the main stem.

Dwarf coconut palm
Microcoelum weddeliana

SUCCESS WITH PALMS

● Do not give palms extreme temperatures. About 15°C (59°F) at night will suit most palms. Winter night temperatures much below 10°C (50°F) or above 21°C (70°F) will damage their fronds.

● Provide good light but avoid strong, direct sunlight as this will burn the fronds. Some palms enjoy a few hours of bright, direct light each day. The parlour palm, *Chamaedorea elegans*, and the kentia palm, *Howeia forsteriana*, will grow well in light to medium shade.

● Provide good drainage to avoid a waterlogged compost. All pots should be well-crocked, with drainage holes and a saucer underneath to collect excess water. Keep the compost slightly moist in winter, but water freely in summer when the compost begins to dry out.

● Palms are sensitive to chemical sprays. Before using any insecticides check that they are suitable for palms. Do not use aerosols near palms, even those for cleaning windows or polishing furniture. Do not use leaf-shine products to clean the leaves; use a soft, damp cloth when the plant is out of strong sunlight.

● Keep palms out of draughts.

● Mist them with clean water, especially in summer. If you mist them in winter, do so in the morning to give the leaves enough time to dry before nightfall.

● Disturb the roots as little as possible. Only repot palms when their roots completely fill the pot.

● Composts and Mixes pp.166–167

The exotic-looking bromeliads originate from the tropics and subtropics of the New World — from South and Central America, and from the southern regions of the United States. Some are epiphytes, growing on trunks or branches of rainforest trees; others are terrestrial, living on the forest floor. Yet others have adapted to more open, rocky terrains, even to desert conditions.

Most of the bromeliads grown as houseplants are epiphytes in the wild. Among the most popular are aechmeas, guzmanias and vrieseas. Non-epiphytes widely grown indoors include cryptanthuses and neoregelias.

The rosettes of many epiphytic bromeliads have a distinctive central urn which in the wild remains full of water and 'catches' airborne organic debris that the

MAKING A BROMELIAD TREE

An attractive focal point in any setting, a bromeliad tree is best suited to epiphytic types, such as urn plants, that grow on trees in the wild and to terrestrial types, such as earth stars, that grow on rocks. Plants secured in crevices will benefit from the accumulation of any water that trickles down the branches.

Remove the bromeliad from its pot and secure sphagnum moss around its roots with plastic covered wire.

Position it in a fork or remove a piece of bark to provide a suitable niche and secure with more wire. Mist the moss frequently until the roots have taken hold. Then mist the plant daily.

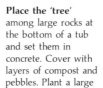

Place the 'tree' among large rocks at the bottom of a tub and set them in concrete. Cover with layers of compost and pebbles. Plant a large bromeliad, such as a vriesea, among the pebbles and secure smaller bromeliads in the forks and crevices of the branches.

• Plants in Profile pp.40–41,
  45–48, 50–52

plant uses for nourishment. Because of this, indoor specimens must have their urns replenished constantly with water and nutrients.

Bromeliads display an extraordinary variety of leaf shapes and formations. But they can generally be divided into those with loose rosettes of narrow leaves, such as billbergias, which are grown mainly for their flowers; and those with striking rosettes of boldly patterned leaves, such as neoregelias, grown mainly for their foliage. At flowering time, some or all of the strap-like leaves of these latter rosettes turn red, pink or purple.

The eye-catching 'blooms' produced by many flowering bromeliads are actually impressive, showy bracts, usually in red or pink. The true flowers, which are rather insignificant, grow from these.

SUCCESS WITH BROMELIADS

- Provide a nighttime temperature of around 10°C (50°F). When starting plants into flower, raise this to 23°C (75°F).
- Provide indirect sunlight in summer but direct sunlight in winter.
- Mist the foliage daily in summer. If misting the foliage in winter, do it early in the day to allow the leaves to dry out before nightfall.
- Feed occasionally while misting – add a dilute fertilizer to the misting water. A dilute fertilizer can also be added to the water used for topping up the urn.
- Do not overwater the compost and make sure it is well drained. Water the plants only when the compost has dried out.
- Keep the urn full of water – never allow it to dry out. In hardwater areas, use rainwater or boiled water that has cooled.
- Replace the water in the urn every 6–8 weeks. Carefully tip the old water out of the urn and pour in fresh. It usually becomes dirtier more quickly in summer than in winter, so check it frequently.
- For those species that do not form urns, keep their compost moist but not continually soaked – waterlogging soon rots the roots.

Use a watering can with a long spout to keep the urn topped up with water and nourishment.

- Humidity pp.156–157
- Feeding pp.162–163

Do not be daunted by the apparent fragility of orchids – many of these beautiful plants are very tolerant and highly resilient. Thanks to careful selection techniques, many are now commonly grown as houseplants. Make sure you give them bright but filtered light and a temperature above 10°C (50°F). Some orchids can tolerate up to 32°C (90°F) if the humidity is kept high. Buy a special potting mix for orchids from your local garden centre and make sure the pot is well drained.

ORCHIDS FOR BEGINNERS

Tiger orchid, *Odontoglossum grande*: Has showy flowers, 15–18 cm across, coloured bright yellow, brownish-red and orange. It needs good light and high humidity in summer and will thrive at a constant 15°C (59°F).

Corsage orchids, *Cattleya spp.*: These offer a range of flowers with frilly-edged, tongue-shaped lips 10–15 cm wide. They need high humidity and a constant temperature in the range 13–15°C (55–59°F).

Slipper orchid, *Paphiopedilum insigne*: Has waxy, slipper-like flowers coloured apple-green, purple-brown and yellow-green. Flowering period is from September to February. This undemanding orchid is ideal for indoor conditions. It needs medium light, normal temperatures and moderate watering.

Coelogyne, *Coelogyne cristata*: Has pure white, fragrant flowers from December to March. This easy-going orchid needs a moist compost in winter. Water more freely in summer. Keep the temperature below 24°C (75°F).

Coelogyne
Coelogyne cristata

Tiger orchid
Odontoglossum grande

INSECT-EATING PLANTS

Acid, boggy and peaty soils lack certain nutrients, particularly nitrogen. To survive in this habitat, some plants have evolved a way of trapping and digesting insects to supplement their diet — their leaves have become carnivorous.

Venus fly trap, *Dionaea muscipula*, (below): Jaw-like, hinged traps have spine-like teeth along outer edges. Hairs near the hinge trigger the jaw's sudden closure when touched. Juices digest the trapped prey and release its protein.

Sundews, *Drosera spp.*: Leaves are covered with red hairs which secrete a sticky, sweet liquid that attracts, adheres to and digests insects. The common sundew, *D. rotundifolia*, needs acid compost, high humidity and a low, but frost-free, temperature.

Pitcher plants: Funnel-shaped leaves contain a liquid which drowns and digests insects. Plants of the genus *Nepenthe* have lids to their pitchers: *Darlingtonia* plants have hoods. They need high humidity, rainwater and a temperature not lower than 7°C (45°F) in winter, but not above 13°C (55°F) in summer.

Venus fly traps need to be grown in sand, sphagnum moss and peat. Place in a sunny position, keep moist and provide winter temperatures of 10–13°C (50–55°F).

SUCCESS WITH ORCHIDS

● Start off by growing orchids you know are easy to grow indoors (see main text).

● Give each orchid individual attention and cater for its own special needs.

● In general, provide a winter nighttime temperature of 10°C (50°F) and a winter day temperature of 15°C (59°F). In summer, raise this to a nighttime 15°C (59°F) and 21°C (70°F) during the day. Remember each orchid has its own temperature preference.

● Provide bright light, with shade at midday on hot summer days. Additional, artificial light may be needed in winter to provide about 12 hours of good light (see pp.152–153)

● Provide high humidity. Mist the leaves in the early morning and stand pots in a tray of pebbles.

● Use special orchid potting compost only.

● Repot only when the pot is totally congested with roots.

● Avoid draughts, but provide good ventilation, especially in summer.

● Feed orchids regularly in summer.

● Keep the compost moist in summer with soft, tepid water. In winter, keep the compost dry.

● Humidity pp.156–157   ● Composts and Mixes pp.166–167

Few houseplants remain immune to attacks by pests, many of which are so small they may at first go unnoticed by the casual observer. They attack plants in different ways. Red spider mites, for example, suck sap from leaves. Weevils chew leaves, stems and even the tips of growing shoots.

It is important to be constantly on the alert so that you can deal promptly not only with pests found indoors all the time, but also those arriving through open windows or on newly-acquired plants.

Established pests are more difficult to eradicate than new arrivals. It makes sense, therefore, to examine plants carefully at least once a month. Isolate any plants showing signs of infestation and take immediate steps to identify and eradicate the culprits.

Diseases almost always result from improper cultivation — overwatering, poor air circulation, excess humidity or very dry air. Such conditions provide fertile ground for infections to take hold and spread.

The microscopic fungi, bacteria and viruses that attack plant cells spread quickly from one plant to another. Remove infected leaves and flowers as soon as you spot them. Cut out any bruised tissue with a sharp knife to stop it becoming infected and dust the cut edge with a fungicidal powder. Chemical sprays also prevent diseases spreading — but always check the label to make sure the product is suitable for the plant.

In the following illustrations, the pests are obviously much enlarged; you may need a magnifying glass to confirm a suspected infestation. Remember that some symptoms may duplicate those arising from other causes — eventual treatment may depend on the results of a process of elimination.

GREENFLY
Aphids that suck sap from soft tissue of most plants, especially shoot tips and flower buds. The honeydew they excrete encourages black mould to grow.
▲ Spray with malathion or dust with derris every 1–2 weeks in summer.

RED SPIDER MITES
Mites that are visible as tiny red dots. They suck sap from leaves and flowers, causing pale yellow mottling.
▲ Spray with malathion or dust with derris.

SCALE INSECTS
Look like tiny, brown discs. Found on undersides of leaves where they suck sap.
▲ Gently wipe off small colonies with a soft cloth dampened with methylated spirit. Spray large colonies with malathion.

MEALY BUGS
Resemble tiny woodlice coated with a white, mealy wax. They suck sap and often form large colonies.
▲ Control as for scale insects.

ROOT MEALY BUGS

Look like mealy bugs. They attack and chew roots, especially those of cacti and succulents, causing discoloration and wilting of leaves.
▲ Drench roots with a solution of malathion.

VINE WEEVILS

Grubs of beetles that chew roots, bulbs and tubers, causing plants to wilt. Adult beetles chew leaves and flowers.
▲ Spray leaves and drench compost with a mixture of thiram, gamma–HCH and rotenone.

THRIPS

(thunder flies): Tiny, black flies that jump from plant to plant, sucking their juices and causing silvery mottling and streaks on leaves and flowers.
▲ Spray with malathion or dust with derris.

CYCLAMEN MITES

Look like specks of dust on the undersides of leaves. Leaves curl, stems twist, flower buds wither and plants are stunted.
▲ Spray with malathion or destroy badly affected plants.

WHITEFLY

Small, white, moth-like flies that cluster under leaves and suck the sap. Their faeces encourage black mould to grow.
▲ Spray with malathion or pyrethrum or dust with derris.

TARSONEMID MITES

Not easy to detect until well established. Feed on youngest growth, causing distorted growth.
▲ Spray slight infestations with malathion; destroy badly affected plants.

LEAFHOPPERS

Adults can jump from one plant to another. They suck sap from the undersides of soft leaves, causing a yellowish or white mottling on top.
▲ Spray with malathion or dust with derris.

STEM AND BULB EELWORMS

Minute, worm-like pests from unsterilized compost that cause plants to soften, distort and to rot.
▲ Never use unsterilized compost. Destroy infested plants.

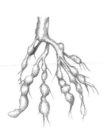

ROOT KNOT EELWORM

Minute, worm-like pests from unsterilized compost that cause swellings and eventual wilting on most plants except bulbs.
▲ Never use unsterilized compost. Destroy infested plants.

WOODLICE

Attack roots, stems and leaves on plants brought indoors from an infected greenhouse.
▲ Spray plants with pirimiphos-methyl.

NARCISSUS FLY MAGGOTS

Tiny maggots tunnel into bulbs especially daffodils, making them soft. Flowers fall and leaves become grass-like.
▲ Destroy infested plants.

CATERPILLARS

Moth or butterfly larvae that feed on leaves, stems, flowers, even roots.
▲ Pick off and kill larvae. Spray with fenitrothion or dust with derris.

SLUGS

These slow-movers chew stems, leaves and flowers at night. They may be brought in by plants standing outside in summer.
▲ Use slug baits or drench compost with metaldehyde formulated as a liquid.

LEAF MINERS

Fly larvae that tunnel into leaves and cause simple, white blotches or long, winding, white lines.
▲ Spray with malathion as soon as tunnels are seen.

PESTICIDES

● All pesticides are lethal. Keep them out of reach of children and animals.

● Systemic pesticides are absorbed by plants and remain in their sap. Once treated, a whole plant will remain deadly to chewing or sucking pests until the poison has worked its way out of the sap.

● Derris and pyrethrum are probably the least powerful and least persistent pesticides. If you keep fish, cover their tank or bowl before dusting with derris.

● Malathion is indiscriminate. It kills many houseplant pests and also damages succulents and ferns.

BOTRYTIS
(grey mould): Grey, fluffy mould over soft parts of leaves, stems, buds and flowers.
▲ Improve ventilation around plant, keep foliage dry and spray with benomyl.
Destroy badly affected plants.

BLACK MOULD
(sooty mould): Fungus that grows on the secretions of greenfly and other sap-sucking insects.
▲ Spray as for greenfly.

BLACK LEG
Cuttings of fleshy plants are susceptible to this disease which makes their bases turn black and rot.
▲ Hormone rooting powder helps ward off attack. Burn infected cuttings.

MILDEW
Fungus that coats or spots leaves with a white powder.
▲ Cut off badly affected leaves, improve air circulation and spray with benomyl.

REMEMBER . . .
● Plants from reputable retail outlets are likely to be free from pests and diseases.
● Inspect all new plants before you buy them. Similarly, inspect any plants you receive as gifts. Keep new arrivals in quarantine for a week or two until you know they are free from disease.
● Do not propagate from infected plants.
● Check your plants regularly. Established pests and diseases are much more difficult to eradicate than newly-arrived ones.
● Regularly mist the leaves of many plants to deter such pests as red spider mites.
● Do not use garden soil as it is likely to contain harmful bacteria and other microorganisms.
● Remove dead flowers and leaves before they attract infections.
● Active pests, such as greenfly, thrips, whitefly or red spider mites, usually affect several plants. Spray all the plants, after first checking that each is tolerant to the spray to be used.
● Slow-moving pests, such as scale insects and mealy bugs, take time to reach other plants. You need not spray all your plants – thoroughly check each one before spraying.
● Follow the manufacturer's instructions to the letter.
● Spray outside, if possible, in a sheltered position.
● Aerosol sprays can damage curtains, furniture, etc. Spray plants in a big plastic bag and leave for 20 mins.

● Humidity pp.156–157   ● Compost and Mixes
● Watering pp.158–161   pp.166–167

HOUSEPLANT
DESIGN

Every houseplant has its own style — a distinctive form, colour, texture or some other feature that underlines its individuality. Because of this, arranging plants in the home becomes a matter of taste: you must match the style of a plant to the context of its surroundings.

Putting the right plant in the right place as well as combining plants in thoughtful arrangements demands only a basic knowledge of the concepts of design. There are few hard-and-fast rules for you to obey because so much of houseplant design is subjective. No one can say to you 'This plant must go here' or 'That plant must go there'. In the end, it is always up to you to decide what looks best and is most workable.

The guidelines outlined in the following pages will help you display your houseplants to best effect. Remember that a houseplant's needs take precedence over aesthetics. First and foremost, each plant must have the right conditions to survive. Do not force a plant to live permanently in conditions it dislikes merely because you think it looks good there. If your designs give a plant 'unnatural' treatment, make sure it has regular 'holidays' in a better position.

Think of houseplants as living décor, focal points of interior design that grow and change. Use their individuality so that they blend with or complement the style in which you have decorated your home or office. There is such a variety of houseplants available that it is not difficult to find plants that fit your design tastes. Use plant colours, contours, outlines, shapes, sizes and patterns to realize some of your ideas in three dimensions.

Make your plants visually interesting. Arrange them in pairs or groups. Try to balance their shapes and sizes, using principles of symmetry and contrast to highlight their individual styles, just as you would with inanimate objects.

Choose a stylish container for each plant to add the finishing touch. As well as using bought containers, you can have fun with home made or improvised ones.

Using spotlights to illuminate individual houseplants is really an optional extra, but if deployed strategically lights can add a new dimension to your designs. A narrow beam from a spotlight can, for instance, create a dramatic interplay of light and shadow on walls and ceilings.

Some plants need to be displayed on their own – their size, shape or colour demands it. But others can be made to work in harmony with each other.

Plants can be grouped to make a variety of pyramids, rectangles (either horizontal or vertical), triangles or even spheres. Whatever shape you choose can be emphasized by a container of suitable proportions.

Remember to choose plants that enjoy the same living conditions. And since plants are continuously growing, you may have to trim or prune them to maintain the group shapes you want.

Try to find shapes that fit in with the style of your room. Formal and high-tec rooms comfortably accommodate plants with sharp outlines, such as mother-in-law's tongue. Rooms with chintz curtains and cottage-style furniture need the soft outlines afforded by either flowering or trailing plants.

DESIGNING WITH SUPPORTS

Houseplant supports can be made from wire, strong plastic or thin, pliable canes in various designs (see below). They can create interesting shapes and visual effects with your small climbers. The stems and leaves of pink jasmine blend well with pliable canes. The sweetheart plant looks good on a plastic trellis.

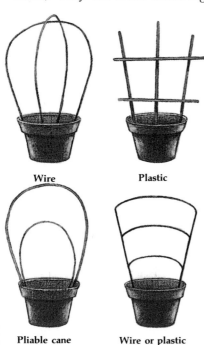

Wire

Plastic

Pliable cane

Wire or plastic

Provide support for pink jasmines at the earliest opportunity before the stems tangle and twist into an unsightly shape. Train the stems around the support and simply let the plant do the rest. Some plants, such as the sweetheart plant, need to have their stems secured to the support. Use soft string or small metal rings and position them just below a leaf-joint.

PYRAMID SHAPES

The symmetry of a pyramid is too precise to be recreated exactly by plants. The best compromise is achieved by a mixture of flowering and foliage plants. In the illustration, the plume-like spires of *Celosia argentea plumosa* create the apex, while the trailing mother of thousands and creeping fig form the sides. As a rule, position the same number of low-growing plants on each side of the central one.

RECTANGULAR SHAPES

Rigid outlines and right angles are rarely seen in the living world of plants. But a group of several similar plants, such as *Sansevieria trifasciata*, may create a shape that is not far removed from a rectangle. The contrived display may be enhanced by placing two plants of the cream-edged variety, 'Laurentii', between two individuals of the type species.

TRIANGULAR SHAPES

Asymmetrical shapes such as this are the most flexible of design forms. While precise triangles cannot be recreated, irregular triangles can be composed by mixing flowering, trailing and large foliage plants. This arrangement leads the eye down the sloping side of the triangle from the rubber plant, to the sweetheart plant, then to the asparagus fern and finally to the iron cross begonia.

• Grooming Houseplants pp.172–175   • Containers pp.206–207

Visual balance is a critical aspect of designing with plants. How the plants strike the eye – whether in relation to each other or to the features in their surroundings – is what matters in houseplant display. Such visual balance can be enhanced or undermined by the plants' containers and by your attention to details such as symmetry.

Plant attributes such as size, shape, texture, leaf or flower colour and density of foliage, all contribute to a plant's 'appearance weight'. This useful, though rather unscientific, term refers to the degree to which plants either attract or distract the eye.

Large plants tend to have more appearance weight than small plants. Yet this is not always true. Large palms, for example, have foliage that allows much of the background to be seen. Consequently, a palm has less appearance weight than a Swiss cheese plant of the same size. Small plants with dense foliage that screens out the background, or striking foliage that distracts the eye, have a greater appearance weight than larger plants with thinner or less dramatic foliage.

When arranging plants in a room, do not think only in terms of each plant's appearance weight. Consider also where to position them – at floor level, on a table or a shelf, or in a hanging basket. Try to balance them in with their surroundings or else make a deliberately contrasting feature of them.

A plant displayed in the centre of a table does not need to be balanced in the same way as plants positioned at floor level. In the mind's eye such a plant becomes identified with the table and ceases to be a feature in its own right. A collection of trailing plants on a shelf becomes part of its background and not a focal point that needs balancing.

Hanging baskets can assume different roles, depending on where you position them. In a corner, away from a door, they produce an asymmetry that does not need to be balanced. But you should use a pair of hanging baskets positioned symmetrically on either side of a window to create the balance that this situation demands.

Symmetry

Asymmetry

Use the features of your room, such as a shelf in front of a mirror, when trying to achieve visual balance. To create an asymmetrical design, balance a tall plant such as a weeping fig with three small plants of the same species, such as creeping figs.

A symmetrical design, using the same mirror and shelf, can be created by positioning two weeping figs as shown here. The eye is drawn between the plants, into the mirror, where the design is enhanced by the symmetrical reflections of the leaves.

SYMMETRY AND ASYMMETRY

To achieve visual balance, you need to take symmetry and asymmetry into account when positioning your plants. Exploit the lines and shapes of the features in your rooms (see above), as well as the attributes of your plants.

Two large rubber plants or kentia palms positioned symmetrically at floor level on either side of a window, large door or alcove are far more effective than a solitary specimen. In the illustration (see far left), a dracaena closely flanked on either side by a spider plant together create a symmetrical design.

Asymmetrical designs can also be visually balanced, but in a different way. In the illustration (see near left), the two spider plants are placed together to one side of the dracaena. To create a visually balanced but asymmetrical design, the spider plants need to be placed a short distance away from the dracaena.

• Designing Shapes pp.200–201   • Contrasts pp.204–205

By introducing contrasts as an element of design, you can add interest to the way your houseplants are displayed. For instance, try combining plants that have contrasting shapes, sizes, textures, colour tones or patterns.

You will need to experiment with a number of different plant combinations before you achieve a pleasing effect. Do not be too ambitious to begin with — try to contrast a single element in one group. For example, compose a group of subtly contrasting textures or else boldly contrasting shapes.

Once you have succeeded in using one contrasting element, introduce another — try arranging groups of contrasting shape and colour. But remember, always keep the groups visually balanced.

Try contrasting the shapes of plants that share the same leaf arrangement, such as the false aralia (*above right*) and the parasol plant (*above left*).

The bold, puckered leaves of the rex begonia (*near left*) juxtaposed with the dainty fronds of the maidenhair fern (*far left*) provide a good contrast of textures.

CONTRASTING SHAPES
There is a wealth of different plant shapes and forms to choose from, including rounded, rosette-forming, upright and umbrella-like. Move your plants around and make contrasting shapes complement each other. Some plants, such as the false aralia and parasol plant, have similar leaf arrangements but contrasting shapes (see illustration left).

CONTRASTING TEXTURES
Puckered, quilted, soft, glossy, hairy, wrinkled, wavy – these are just some of the leaf textures you can employ to great effect. Appearance weight (pp.200–201) also contributes to the overall texture of a plant. For example, the wispy nature of the maidenhair fern provides a striking contrast to the denser rex begonia (see illustration below left).

CONTRASTING LEAF SIZES
The leaves of houseplants range enormously in size. For instance, the leaves of baby's tears are only 5 mm across, while those of the tree philodendron reach 45 cm across. When using differences in leaf size as a design theme, choose plants with the same basic leaf shape, such as oval or heart-shaped (see illustration above right).

CONTRASTING TONES
Juxtaposing plants whose leaves have the same colour tone or hue, tends to make the leaf shapes indistinct to the eye. By grouping plants whose foliage is sufficiently different in tone, you can give greater effect to the pattern and shape of the leaves (see illustration right).

Choose plants with the same leaf shape to highlight the contrast in leaf size. This theme works well with the crystal anthurium (*above right*) and the emerald ripple (*above left*).

When adjacent plants have contrasting tones of the same colour, the eye focuses more easily on leaf shapes and patterns, as with the bird's nest fern (*above left*) and rabbit tracks (*above right*).

• Designing Shapes
pp.200–201

• Balancing Groups
pp.202–203

No matter how healthy your plants may be, they will not look their best in ugly or dirty pots that stand on old or chipped saucers. Plants need eye-catching containers to emphasize their good looks.

Any container should be in proportion to the plant. Small plants need containers of roughly equal height; let your eye judge container sizes for taller plants.

A container's colour and shape should complement those of the plant. Avoid colours that clash and shapes that jar unless you want a bizarre effect. Well-defined shapes and subdued colours will work effectively in most settings.

The plant, together with its container, should suit their chosen position. Try to think in terms of style and materials — wicker baskets suit wooden tables, but an art deco container will look out of place in a cottage-style room.

An umbrella stand makes an interesting alternative to a hanging basket for trailing plants such as the rat's tail cactus (*above*). Remember to fill the stand with stones or small bricks so that its top and the rim of the pot are level.

Complement a natural surface such as wood with a container also made of a natural material. For example, place a wicker basket full of low-growing plants, such as painted net leaf, on a wooden table (*left*).

In a cottage-style setting, try echoing the patterns of the container and your furnishings with an aptly chosen plant. The common ivy (*left*) is echoed in the design on the Victorian wash bowl and also on the table cloth.

Home made containers provide intriguing opportunities for design. For example, a painted, metal wastepaper basket makes a splendid container for a tall, spiky yucca plant. Remember to drill drainage holes in the base of the container and place it in a metal baking tray to catch the excess water.

IMPROVISED CONTAINERS

Containers can be expensive, so think carefully when making your choices. Alternatively, you could seek out everyday objects − buckets, wastepaper baskets, casserole dishes, biscuit tins, copper mugs − and convert them into plant containers.

Remember you must make sure your container is waterproof, otherwise you may find ugly marks on your tables and shelves, or even indelible stains on the carpet. You can line wicker baskets with polythene, for instance, and coat the inside of unglazed china pots with polyurethane.

• Designing Shapes
pp.200–201

Inventive use of artificial lighting can add a new dimension to the designs you are able to create with your indoor plants. Always use a lighting arrangement that enhances the style of your room as well as your plants.

Experiment with lighting your plants from one direction – from above or below, from the side, or from the front or back. Try to accentuate a particular aspect of a plant – its shape, colour or texture. You may find you can also create dramatic contrasts of light and shadow by using your plant silhouettes to enliven neglected corners and bare walls.

Lights with tungsten filament bulbs are the most popular form of spotlighting. Try to set up spotlights so that they can be moved up and down or turned to any angle. This will give you more flexibility in choosing the lighting you want. A word of warning: do not place a spotlight too near to a plant or the heat will burn the leaves. As a rule, a 100-watt bulb should be 50 cm or more away from the leaves of a plant.

Downlighting reduces a plant in size, while shadows cast on the wall and the surface on which the plant is standing extend the plant's outline. Create downlighting by positioning a spotlight on the ceiling, or high up on a wall, above and to one side of the plant. Angle the light so that it shines down on the plant, highlighting the upper leaf surfaces and throwing the rest of the plant into shadow.

Sidelighting a plant
accentuates leaf colour
and texture. When a
small plant is
positioned on a glossy
surface, leaf reflections
and the shadow cast
by the container can
also add interest.

**Uplighting creates
shadows** that appear
to inflate the scale and
size of a plant. Either
mount the light low
on the wall so you can
vary the angle of its
beam, or use an
uplighter – a lamp
with a flat base which
stands on the floor
and allows the beam
to shine vertically
upward.

• Light pp.150–153

Annual: A plant grown from seed that produces flowers and returns to seed within a year.

Bigeneric hybrid: A plant produced by crossing two plants from different genera. This is indicated by an '×' before its scientific name, e.g. × *Fatshedera lizei*.

Bonemeal: A fertilizer rich in phosphates.

Bract: A modified, often conspicuous, leaf usually asssociated with the flowering parts of a plant. May be leaf- or petal-like, green or other colours.

Chlorophyll: The green pigment present in most plants which traps energy from sunlight during photosynthesis.

Corolla: The part of a flower composed of fused or partially fused petals. Usually coloured (i.e. not green).

Forcing: Encouraging plants, especially bulbs, to flower earlier than they would do naturally.

Form: A synonym for variety.

Genus: The botanical classification given to a group of plants with characteristics in common. The first part of a plant's scientific name indicates its genus. E.g. daffodils belong to the genus *Narcissus*. In nature, plants from different genera cannot normally breed together successfully (i.e. to produce fertile offspring).

Hybrid: A plant resulting from a cross between two distinct species, varieties, cultivars or subspecies. This is indicated by a '×' placed between the generic and specific parts of the scientific name, e.g. *Begonia* × *tuberhybrida*.

Hydroponics: The cultivation of plants in water, without compost but with plant food added in controlled amounts.

Lobe: A rounded or pointed projection of a leaf or petal.

Offset: A shoot produced from the base of a plant which is a small replica of its parent. If detached, it will grow into a new plant.

Offshoot: Either a shoot arising from another shoot, or a synonym frequently used for an offset.

Perennial: A plant that lives for at least three years.

Photosynthesis: The manufacture of carbohydrates by means of a series of chemical reactions involving sunlight, chlorophyll, water and carbon dioxide.

Phototropism: The response of plants to light. Most stems, for example, grow toward a source of light and are said to be positively phototropic.

Propagation: Increasing plants, either by sowing seeds, dividing established plants or detaching parts of plants and encouraging them to develop roots.

Rhizome: A swollen stem that stores food and grows, either partially or wholly, under the compost.

Rootball: The roots of a potted plant and the compost that surrounds them.

Rosette: A number of leaves radiating in a circle from a central point.

Sepal: One of several modified leaves that form the outermost part of a flower and protect the petals and the reproductive organs. Usually green, but may be brightly coloured.

Spadix: A fleshy flower spike with tiny flowers embedded in shallow pits. The spike is a feature of plants belonging to the arum family (Araceae).

Spathe: The large bract or modified leaf that surrounds the spadix of flowers belonging to the arum family (Araceae).

Species: An individual plant or a closely associated group of plants in the same genus which share almost identical characteristics. Members of the same species can breed together successfully. A species is designated by a two-word scientific name, e.g. *Philodendron scandens*, of which the first word is the name of the genus.

Sphagnum moss: A moss that can absorb and hold water. In a decomposed state it is a major ingredient of peat and is used to retain moisture around the roots and stems of plants.

Spur: A hollow, tubular outgrowth of a petal or sepal which may produce nectar.

Stamen: The male reproductive part of a flower, consisting of pollen-bearing lobes, the anthers, supported on filaments.

Stigma: The exposed tip of the female reproductive organs on which is collected pollen.

Style: The stalk of the female reproductive system that supports the stigma and connects it to the ovary.

Sucker: A shoot arising from the base of a plant below compost level.

Transpiration: The loss of water vapour from a plant, particularly through minute pores in the leaves. The rate of transpiration varies with the time of day and environmental conditions.

Tuber: An underground storage organ that enables a plant to overwinter or live through periods of drought. Also an organ from which a plant can be propagated.

Variety: A subdivision of a species in which individual plants differ from the original in features such as size, colour, variegations, etc. Varieties originate in the wild. Plants that have been raised in cultivation are called cultivars. The name of a variety usually follows the species name and is printed in roman type, e.g. *Sansevieria trifasciata* 'Laurentii'.

Whorl: Flowers or leaves that grow from the same point and are arranged so that they radiate like wheel spokes.

CLIMBING HOUSEPLANTS

Arrowhead vine (p.116)
Begonia vine (p.61)
Black gold philodendron (p.101)
Blushing philodendron (p.101)
Common ivy (p.113)
Devil's ivy (p.100)
Elephant's ear philodendron (p.101)
Grape ivy (p.61)
Ivy tree (p.124)
Kangaroo vine (p.61)
Madagascar jasmine (p.13)
Pink jasmine (p.117)
Primrose jasmine (p.117)
Sweetheart plant (p.101)
Swiss cheese plant (p.105)

TRAILING AND CASCADING HOUSEPLANTS/FOLIAGE

Asparagus fern (p.64)
Burro's tail (p.144)
Button fern (p.65)
Creeping fig (p.108)
Devil's ivy (p.100)
Ladder fern (p.137)
Maidenhair fern (p.136)
Mother of thousands (p.15)
Painted net leaf (p.76)
Plume asparagus (p.64)
Silvery inch plant (p.68)
Snakeskin plant (p.76)
Spider plant (p.60)
String of beads (p.134)
Sweetheart plant (p.101)

TRAILING AND CASCADING HOUSEPLANTS/FLOWERING

Basket begonia (p.122)
Christmas cactus (p.142)
Crab cactus (p.142)
Easter cactus (pp.142–143)
Goldfish plant (pp.66–67)
Ivy-leaved pelargonium (p.102)
Rat's tail cactus (pp.138–139)

ARCHITECTURAL HOUSEPLANTS

Canary date palm (p.133)
Coral berry (p.85)
Dragon tree (p.96)
False aralia (p.57)
False castor oil plant (p.125)
Ivy tree (p.124)
Kentia palm (p.129)
Norfolk Island pine (p.128)
Parasol plant (p.104)
Rubber plant (pp.108–109)
Sentry palm (p.129)
Silk oak (p.145)
Spanish bayonet (p.49)
Spineless yucca (p.49)
Swiss cheese plant (p.105)
Umbrella plant (p.56)
Weeping fig (p.108)

EASY-TO-GROW HOUSEPLANTS

Asparagus fern (p.64)
Common ivy (p.113)
Daffodil (pp.38–39)
False castor oil plant (p.125)
Grape ivy (p.61)
Ivy tree (p.124)
Kangaroo vine (p.61)
Mother-in-law's tongue (p.53)
Parlour palm (p.132)
Piggy-back plant (p.112)
Rubber plant (pp.108–109)
Silk oak (p.145)
Spider plant (p.60)
Striped inch plant (p.68)
Umbrella plant (p.56)
Wandering Jew (p.68)

SCENTED HOUSEPLANTS

Coral berry (p.85)
Daffodil (pp.38–39)
Hyacinth (pp.34–35)
Lemon-scented geranium (p.102)
Madagascar jasmine (p.13)
Miniature wax plant (p.13)
Peppermint geranium (p.21)
Persian violet (p.80)
Pink jasmine (p.117)
Rose geranium (p.20)
String of beads (p.134)

HOUSEPLANTS THAT TOLERATE FUMES

Cast iron plant (p.93)
False castor oil plant (p.125)
Ivy tree (p.124)
Mother-in-law's tongue (p.53)
Rubber plant (pp.108–109)
Screw pine (p.36)
Urn plant (pp.46–47)

SENSITIVE HOUSEPLANTS

(Unsuitable for beginners because difficult to grow or intolerant of low temperatures)

Arrowhead vine (p.116)
Chenille plant (p.73)
Croton (pp.54–55)
Crystal anthurium (p.90)
Cyclamen (pp.126–127)
False aralia (p.57)
Flamingo flower (p.90)
Goldfish plant (pp.66–67)
Maidenhair fern (p.136)
Never never plant (p.86)
Ornamental pepper (p.18)
Painted net leaf (p.76)
Painter's palette (pp.90–91)
Peacock plant (p.88)
Rose of China (pp.110–111)
Zebra plant (p.88)

HOUSEPLANTS WITH WHITE FLOWERS

African violet (pp.82–83)
Amaryllis (pp.42–43)
Azalea (pp.74–75)
Busy lizzie (pp.70–71)
Chrysanthemum (pp.58–59)
Cineraria (pp.134–135)
Coral berry (p.85)
Cyclamen (pp.126–127)
Daffodil (pp.38–39)
Emerald ripple (p.84)
Flaming katy (p.77)
Hyacinth (pp.34–35)
Peace lily (p.97)
Pelargonium (pp.102–103)
Poinsettia (pp.62–63)
Spider plant (p.60)
Yucca (p.49)

HOUSEPLANTS WITH WHITE/CREAM/SILVER VARIEGATIONS

Aluminium plant (p.72)
Arrowhead vine (p.116)
Canary Island ivy (p.19)
Candle flower (p.14)
Chinese evergreen (p.92)
Crystal anthurium (p.90)
Dragon tree (p.96)
Dumb cane (p.89)
Partridge-breasted aloe (p.44)
Screw pine (p.36)
Silver lace fern (p.140)
Spider plant (p.60)
Striped inch plant (p.16)
Urn plant (pp.46–47)
Zebra plant (pp.106–107)

HOUSEPLANTS WITH YELLOW FLOWERS

Begonia (pp.122–123)
Chrysanthemum (pp.58–59)
Daffodil (pp.38–39)
Flaming katy (p.77)
Hyacinth (pp.34–35)
Primrose jasmine (p.117)
Rose of China (pp.110–111)
Slipper plant (pp.118–119)
Zebra plant (pp.106–107)

HOUSEPLANTS WITH YELLOW VARIEGATIONS

Century plant (p.25)
Croton (pp.54–55)
Devil's ivy (p.100)
Goldenheart ivy (p.19)
Mother-in-law's tongue (p.53)
Spotted flowering maple (p.20)

HOUSEPLANTS WITH PINK FLOWERS

Angel's tears (p.41)
Azalea (pp.74–75)
Burro's tail (p.144)
Busy lizzie (pp.70–71)
Chrysanthemum (pp.58–59)
Cyclamen (pp.126–127)
Hydrangea (pp.94–95)
Pelargonium (pp.102–103)
Rat's tail cactus (pp.138–139)
Urn plant (pp.46–47)
Wax begonia (p.122)

HOUSEPLANTS WITH RED FLOWERS

Amaryllis (pp.42–43)
Azalea (pp.74–75)
Begonia (pp.122–123)
Busy lizzie (pp.70–71)
Chenille plant (p.73)
Chrysanthemum (pp.58–59)
Cineraria (pp.134–135)
Cyclamen (pp.126–127)
Easter cactus (pp.142–143)
Fairy primrose (pp.114–115)
Flaming katy (p.77)
Flaming sword (p.40)
Gloxinia (pp.130–131)
Goldfish plant (pp.66–67)
Hot water plant (pp.78–79)
Hyacinth (pp.34–35)
Painter's palette (pp.90–91)
Pelargonium (pp.102–103)
Poinsettia (pp.62–63)
Rose of China (pp.110–111)
Slipper plant (pp.118–119)

HOUSEPLANTS WITH RED/ PINK VARIEGATIONS

Blushing bromeliad (pp.50–51)
Croton (pp.54–55)
Fingernail plant (p.50)
Herringbone plant (pp.86–87)
Japanese sedum (p.15)
Mother of thousands (p.15)
Ornamental pepper (p.18)
Painted net leaf (p.76)
Polka dot plant (p.81)
Ti log plant (pp.98–99)

HOUSEPLANTS WITH BLUE/ PURPLE FLOWERS

African violet (pp.82–83)
Cineraria (pp.134–135)
Coral berry (p.46)
Cyclamen (pp.126–127)
Fairy primrose (pp.114–115
Gloxinia (pp.130–131)
Hot water plant (pp.78–79)
Hyacinth (pp.34–35)
Hydrangea (pp.94–95)
Persian violet (p.80)
Pineapple plant (p.52)

HOUSEPLANTS WITH PURPLE ON THEIR LEAVES

Begonia vine (p.18)
Boat lily (p.37)
Metallic leaf begonia (p.120)
Plush vine (p.17)
Prayer plant (pp.86–87)
Purple heart (p.17)
Purple passion vine (p.16)
Silvery inch plant (p.68)
Velvet plant (p.16)

HOUSEPLANTS FOR BRIGHT SUNNY WINDOWS

Amaryllis (pp.42–43)
Burro's tail (p.144)
Easter cactus (pp.142–143)
Partridge-breasted aloe (p.44)
Pelargonium (pp.102–103)
Pink jasmine (p.117)
Rat's tail cactus (pp.138–139)

Also recommended:
Goat's horn cactus (*Astrophytum capricorne*) (p.185)
Hedgehog cactus (*Echinocereus pectinatus*) (p.185)
Jade tree (*Crassula argentea*) (p.185)
Living stones (eg. *Lithops fulleri*)
Old man cactus (*Cephalocereus senilis*)
Painted lady (*Echeveria derenbergii*)

HOUSEPLANTS FOR BRIGHT SUNLIGHT, BUT NOT FULL SUN

(Between 1 and 2 metres from a bright, sunny window)

Aluminium plant (p.72)
Bromeliads (pp.190–191)
Common ivy (p.113)
Cyclamen (pp.126–127)
Devil's ivy (p.100)
Dumb cane (p.89)
Emerald ripple (p.84)
False aralia (p.57)
Flamingo flower (p.90)
Goldfish plant (pp.66–67)
Painter's palette (pp.90–91)
Parasol plant (p.104)
Philodendrons (p.101)
Rex begonia (p.120)
Swiss cheese plant (p.105)

HOUSEPLANTS FOR SOME DIRECT, BUT NOT FULL, SUN

(Within a metre of a bright, sunny window)

African violet (pp.82–83)
Busy lizzie (pp.70–71)
Chrysanthemum (pp.58–59)
Croton (pp.54–55)
Mother-in-law's tongue (p.53)
Poinsettia (pp.62–63)
Rubber plant (pp.108–109)
Shrimp plant (p.69)
Silvery inch plant (p.68)
Spider plant (p.60)
Ti log plant (pp.98–99)
Wandering Jew (p.68)

HOUSEPLANTS FOR SEMI-SHADE

(Farther than 2 metres from a bright, sunny window)

Cast iron plant (p.93)
Chinese evergreen (p.92)
Common ivy (p.113)
False castor oil plant (p.125)
Ferns (pp.186–187)
Ivy tree (p.124)
Mother-in-law's tongue (p.53)
Painted net leaf (p.76)
Piggy-back plant (p.112)
Prayer plant (pp.86–87)
Sweetheart plant (p.101)

HOUSEPLANTS FOR ROOMS WITH LITTLE SUNLIGHT

Bird's nest fern (p.141)
Cast iron plant (p.93)
Chinese evergreen (p.92)
Ferns (pp.186–187)
Hen and chicken fern (p.141)
Mother-in-law's tongue (p.53)
Painted net leaf (p.76)
Sweetheart plant (p.101)

HOUSEPLANTS FOR COOL ROOMS

(Rooms usually 2–7°C [35–45°F])

Cacti (pp.184–185)
Cast iron plant (p.93)
Cineraria (pp.134–135)
Common ivy (p.113)
Cyclamen (pp.126–127)
False castor oil plant (p.125)
Hydrangea (pp.94–95)
Ivy tree (p.124)
Mother of thousands (p.15)
Piggy-back plant (p.112)
Purple heart (p.17)
Spider plant (p.60)
Succulents (pp.184–185)

METRIC CONVERSION TABLE

6 mm	0.25 in
12 mm	0.5 in
18 mm	0.75 in
2.5 cm	1 in
5 cm	2 in
7.5 cm	3 in
10 cm	4 in
12.5 cm	5 in
15 cm	6 in
20 cm	8 in
25 cm	10 in
30 cm	12 in
40 cm	16 in
45 cm	18 in
50 cm	20 in
75 cm	30 in
100 cm (1 m)	40 in

Numerals in italics refer to illustrations in the Plant Identification section.
Numerals in bold type refer to illustrations in the Plants in Profile section.

ACKNOWLEDGEMENTS

ILLUSTRATORS:
Karen Daws, 172–5;
Gill Elsbury, 64–5, 88–9,
96–7, 100–1, 108–9, 112–13,
116–17, 124–5, 128–9,
132–3, 136–7, 140–1,
158–61, 168–71, 176–81,
204–9;
Anthony Morris, 118–19,
144–5;
Jane Pickering, 34–41, 44–9,
52–63, 66–9, 72–3, 76–85,
90–3, 102–7, 110–11,
114–15, 120–3, 126–7,
130–1, 134–5, 142–3,
148–53, 162–5, 182–7,
190–3, 200–3;
Anette Robinson, 42–3,
50–1, 70–1, 74–5, 86–7,
94–5, 98–9, 138–9;
Cheryl Wilbraham, 9–31,
156–7, 188–9, 194–7.

INDEX: Don Binney